4
CG

There Once Was a Time

Piero Ventura

There Once Was a Time

G. P. Putnam's Sons   New York

Copyright © 1986 by Arnoldo Mondadori Editore S.p.A., Milano
English translation copyright © 1987 by Arnoldo Mondadori
Editore S.p.A., Milano
All rights reserved. Published simultaneously in Canada by
General Publishing Co. Limited, Toronto. Originally published
in Italy by Arnoldo Mondadori Editore, 1986, under the title
Com'era una volta. English translation by James Ramsay.
Translation adapted by Judith St. George
Printed and bound in Spain by Artes Gráficas Toledo S.A.
Book design by Martha Rago
Library of Congress Cataloging-in-Publication Data
Ventura, Piero.   There once was a time. Translation of:
Com'era una volta.
Summary: A world history presenting various aspects of life during
particular periods of history, focusing heavily on Europe, in a manner
allowing the reader to make topical comparisons between the periods.
1. World history—Juvenile literature.   [1. World history.
2. Civilization—History.   3. Europe—History] I. Title.
D21.V37313   1987   909   86-25237   ISBN 0-399-21356-2
First impression
D. L. TO:1874-1986

Contents

Key

 Society, forms of government, institutions, economy

 Houses, building methods, architectural styles, the growth of cities

 Agriculture, life and work on the land, food production

 Arts and trades, the work of craftsmen and laborers, materials, methods, products

 Trading and trade routes, merchants, markets

 Dress, fashion, tastes

 Roads, transport, travel

 Inventions, technology, sources of energy

 Organization of armies, warfare, the life of the soldier, arms, weapons, uniforms

Introduction

We are often told that once upon a time there lived a powerful queen, or that there was once a great poet, or a knight-errant. But along with their exploits, what we would really like to know is what their houses were like, or their hometowns, what sort of world they lived in, and just exactly how things used to be.

In history books we read about wars and battles, peoples and kings, great artists and famous cities. But we rarely hear about the details that make these things seem real—what people wore, how they traveled, where they lived, and how they earned a living. If we had a more complete picture, perhaps we would be able to understand better why things happened the way they did, and what influenced leaders in making their decisions.

Imagine that history is like a giant knapsack that could be carried around. Each period of time, group of people, or place on the globe could be taken out and laid on the table. This is what this book is all about—a sample of the stories history has to offer, waiting for the reader to choose.

Each chapter covers nine aspects of a particular era, which can be read together for an overview of how life was at the time. Or the reader can choose particular subjects such as society, fashion, art, and agriculture, and look at how they differ over time and how important they were at every stage in history. This book can, therefore, be read in two ways: first as a guide to different periods in history, and second as an introduction to various aspects of life through the ages.

Special topics discussed within each chapter are marked with symbols that are explained on the facing page. The periods covered are introduced in the chapter title and a chart at the back of the book shows exactly where to find each subject at any given time in history.

The Ancient World

Primitive nomadic tribes chose their chieftains for their courage, knowledge, and leadership ability. Not only were these chiefs familiar with the tribal gods, and able to guide their people by the stars, but they also knew where to lead their tribes to find food and shelter. Because their constant search for food involved the whole tribe, no roles were assigned to any one individual or group, other than the women who cared for very young children and remained in the tents.

Gradually these wandering tribes settled in the fertile valleys of the great rivers, where they began to till the soil and establish towns. In the Nile Valley, different settlements, located in both Lower and Upper Egypt, eventually united into a single kingdom ruled by *pharaohs*. The cities on the Tigris River and the Euphrates River also came under the control of a single ruler, the Assyrian king Sargon II, while in Asia Minor the Hittite kings reigned. Western civilization as we know it was founded on these three great, ancient, economically efficient empires, each of which was organized into a rigid social hierarchy.

The social structure of these civilizations was thought to be divinely ordained. The Egyptian pharaoh, like the king of Babylon, represented the divinity, and his life-

Pharaoh

Royal succession of the pharaoh was determined through the pharaoh's mother, who was believed to have conceived the pharaoh by the supreme god, Ammon. The responsibility of acting as "divine woman" and conceiving the next pharaoh was then passed on to a daughter (often adopted) who in turn became the pharaoh's wife.

Priests

Soldiers

Civil servants of various ranks

In Egypt, showmen and merchants were considered somewhat special, the showmen because of their artistic talents, and the merchants because of their resourcefulness in traveling and establishing contacts with distant places in Asia and Africa.

long reign was based on, and directed by, established religious rituals. Priests, therefore, constituted an immensely powerful class, controlling not only these rituals, but the fate of the throne and the succession of the dynasties as well.

The military also held a key position in the state, providing the force necessary to win and keep the king's position. Of course, their loyalty to the king, the supreme head of the armed forces, had to be unwavering. Equally important to the structure of the state were the civil servants, a powerful bureaucracy that ran the government and oversaw agricultural production, the state's basic source of wealth.

Only the existence of huge numbers of slaves could support all these "nonproductive" social classes. Slave labor also enabled the state to build great monuments, the pyramids, palaces, and temples of those ancient empires.

During the first millennium B.C., a new civilization with a different social structure grew up on the shores of the Mediterranean, in Greece. In contrast to Egyptian rulers, no one man was able to unite all the city-states of ancient Greece into a single kingdom, with the exception of the Spartan monarchs, who held limited power. Instead, the governments of these city-states were controlled by the wealthiest and most powerful families. These aristocrats met in council to elect ruling magistrates, such as the *archons* in Athens, who held power for a fixed period of time. Beginning with Pericles in fifth century B.C. Athens, people who did administrative work were paid, opening those positions to everyone, not just the wealthy classes.

Long, drawn-out debates and fierce competition within governments sometimes gave power-hungry individuals, *tyrants,* an excuse to seize control, supposedly to avoid civil disorder. But plots to displace or even kill these tyrants were common and came to be considered acts of heroism.

Because Greece was politically fragmented and had little real military strength, it was threatened with invasion by Persia more than once. Eventually, Greece had to recognize the authority of the son of Philip of Macedon, Alexander the Great, who was the ambitious leader of a powerful army. In 146 B.C., Greece fell to the Romans almost without a struggle.

Women, who were excluded from all public life in "democratic" Greece, were not even allowed to watch athletes compete in the Olympic games. Actually there were few truly free men in Greece; the perioeci, *who carried on trade, and* helots, *who worked in the fields, were virtual slaves.*

Because the nomadic tribes were constantly on the move in search of food, they lived in tents made of woven straw or animal skins which were easy to take apart and transport. They would take shelter in caves or under trees, using weapons and fire to protect themselves from dangerous animals.

At regular intervals, the nomadic tribes returned to special sites, perhaps where their ancestors were buried, or where they had placed a god's altar-stone, or where they performed hunting and fertility rites. At these gatherings, goods were exchanged and marriages arranged. In time, these shrines and burial places where the tribes met, worshiped their gods, and bought and sold goods became the nuclei of towns. In the center, on a raised site, were the two structures that embodied the tribe's history—the temple where the gods dwelt and the palace of the king.

The nomads, who gradually became herdsmen, found that migrating with cattle and flocks was impossible. At first they sought pasturelands and then, as they became serious farmers, they settled in hut villages. The earliest houses were simple enclosures of rough stonework or straw mixed with dried mud, with roofs of matting and reeds supported by branches. The fire, which was usually outside the hut, was always kept lit, since it was so difficult to start up. Needing a constant source of water, settlements tended to grow up around a river, spring, or well. In Egyptian villages, the children played safely inside the walls while the women prepared food and drink, made jars to be used for storage, cut animal skins, and wove fibers for clothes.

Domesticated animals such as oxen and camels, which were used for work, and pigs, which served a hygienic function by eating refuse, lived alongside the human community. Cats and even snakes were kept as protection against mice and other rodents attracted to food stored for the seasons in which crops couldn't be grown. Dogs too lived alongside of man as both working partners and friends.

Brick was the great invention of ancient builders, and whole cities were constructed of small crude bricks made of clay that was baked in the sun. Great mounds of brick ruins which survive to this day hint at the grandeur that was Babylon.

The stone columns of ancient Greece imitated earlier buildings that had been supported by wooden frames. Because the Greeks used stone, many of their monuments are still standing. Worshipers met outside for sacrifices and prophetic rites, and thus Greek temples contained only statues of the gods.

Gateway to the sacred enclosure of an Egyptian temple

Entrance portico, or pronaos, of a Greek Ionic-style temple

A group of buildings made of bricks covered with mud and straw

Permanent cities with surrounding walls offered a society more structure and safety. At the same time this was a departure from the "freedom" and adaptability of a nomadic way of life.
Although they are much rarer than in ancient times, nomadic tribes still exist today in parts of Africa, North America, and the Middle East.

If we consider how long the human race has been around, the evolution of agriculture 10,000 years ago is a relatively modern development. The idea for sowing seeds probably came from noticing that plants always grew wherever seeds had been discarded. Where groups of people stayed in one place for a time, gardens with naturally selected food crops were cultivated around the camp. Certainly it was easier to collect supplies of grain and fruit by growing them than by constantly moving around to find them elsewhere.

The development of agriculture was a milestone in civilization. As agricultural techniques were perfected, more and more people could be fed and man's place in nature became more secure. Agriculture was the basis on which the wealth of the ancient civilizations of the Mediterranean and the Near East was founded.

Like everything else in these societies, agriculture was distributed from the top down, with the state staking claim on all produce, leaving the farmers barely enough food on which to survive. On the other hand, the state did much to encourage agriculture, such as build canal systems, so that there would be enough produce to feed the entire population.

Farmer with a hoe and his Egyptian overseer

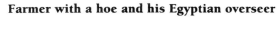

Prehistoric man, who realized that the land had to be tilled to be productive, invented first the hoe and then the plow. Because something larger and sharper than bare hands was needed to harvest crops, early rough flint tools were developed. These gradually evolved into the iron sickles that were used in Egyptian and Babylonian times.

12

Much of a woman's time was spent preparing and preserving food. Ancient Egyptian carvings show women baking bread and straining barley to make beer. Once animals were tamed and raised domestically, they were harnessed for pulling loads; they also became a source of wool, leather, and food such as milk and eggs.

The regular flooding of the Nile carried fertile mud into the fields, guaranteeing two harvests a year. For irrigation, water had to be diverted from rivers and channeled through the fields, a system at which the Babylonians, expert hydraulic engineers, excelled. In less fortunate places, wells had to be dug and water drawn up in animal-skin buckets by means of a lever device called a shaduf, which is still used in Africa today.

13

Fragments of pottery have always played an important role in the search to understand the life of ancient peoples. The ability to model and bake clay is one of mankind's oldest skills: the raw material is found almost everywhere; it is easy to shape and does not require baking at a high temperature.

The fine decoration and durability of a good deal of ancient pottery indicate that a potter had to know his materials and the techniques of firing, as well as be a skilled and accomplished artist. The craftsmen who worked with more difficult materials such as metal were even more highly trained. Archaeological evidence shows that from the earliest times, craftsmen skilled in metal, clay, cloth, leather, and dyes worked alongside the farmers, who were the vast majority of the population.

Some of the beautifully made work that has survived shows the technical mastery achieved by the court craftsmen of ancient times. Because everything was handmade and demanded a good deal of time and effort, only strict discipline and constant refining could have produced work of such high quality.

· The production of certain materials was concentrated in specific areas. Metalwork, for instance, was done close to mines, and many crafts—such as the manufacture of Attic pottery around Athens and of purple dye in Phoenicia—were carried on where the particular techniques originally developed. Trade, especially in valuable metalwork, was vigorous among the various cultures, particularly since the Mediterranean has always been relatively easy to navigate. Cyprus is actually named after the copper that was mined there.

Because their scarcity made them precious, metals were first used only for jewelry, statues, and weapons, and not for tools.

14

The development of the art of pottery

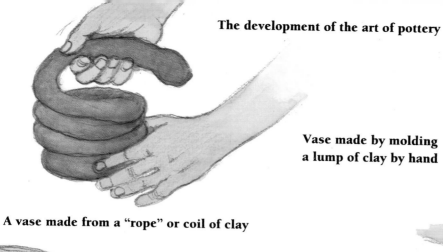

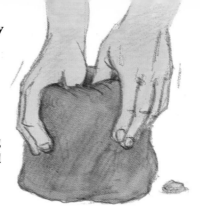

**Vase made by molding
a lump of clay by hand**

A vase made from a "rope" or coil of clay

Vases made on two types of turntables. On the left is a simple plate turntable, and on the right are two disks joined at the hub. Both turntables are worked by hand.

Primitive skills such as chipping flints and modeling clay led to the first "machines," which cut down on labor and improved the quality of what was being produced. The potter's wheel, which was originally turned by hand and then by foot in order to leave both hands free, was already in use by the fourth millennium B.C. The bow drill (see page 22) was used in ancient Egypt, while Iron Age Europe was already working with the hand-operated lathe around 700 B.C.

Because Syria was midway between the great empires of the Near East, it was the trade crossroads of ancient times. All roads led there, from the Assyro-Babylonian cities, from the Hittite civilization of Asia Minor, from Egypt. Here too passed the nomadic Bedouin caravans of the Arabian desert.

Crete, a dry, mountainous island of crowded cities and towns and little agriculture, depended almost entirely on trade for its survival. Like Syria, Crete occupied a central position; and for many centuries the island controlled sea traffic in the Mediterranean. Although Egyptian inscriptions mention that Cretans brought tribute in the form of merchandise, these goods were in fact the results of trade.

The Phoenician cities, set like jewels in the coastline of what is now mountainous Lebanon, communicated with each other by sea. Almost the entire Phoenician populace lived off maritime trade in the Mediterranean.

Surprisingly, trade during those ancient times involved mostly luxury items such as valuable cloth, oint-ments, and perfumes, not everyday goods as might be expected. Transportation was so difficult and expensive that merchants preferred to deal in the least bulky and most valuable goods.

Merchandise was transported in short stages, no matter what distance it had to travel; so the sooner it could be sold, the greater the profit would be. Each area protected its own traders, leaving outsiders vulnerable to attack and robbery. Markets, which were held outdoors in squares and at gateways, displayed all sorts of strange and wonderful items such as ivory, ostrich eggs from Egypt, and lapis lazuli from Afghanistan.

The slave trade flourished. Slaves were tied and bound, stripped half-naked to show their muscles or physical attractiveness, and exhibited in public squares, where they were offered for sale with shouts and crude jokes like any other merchandise.

Writing became a necessity as trade flourished. When writing first began, it was used solely for recording warehouse stocks, accounts, and movements of goods.

Greek vases, with their beautiful painted figures, were highly prized luxury items. Archaeologists have found them in all areas of the Mediterranean.

A vase, or lekythos   **An amphora, a vessel with two handles**   **A pitcher, or oenochoë**

Phoenician and Palestinian coastal towns were the meeting places of the Asian caravan routes and the sea-lanes of the Mediterranean. Both the Phoenicians and the Palestinians kept accurate records of all the goods bought and sold in their warehouses.

In ancient times, men's and women's fashions changed slowly. In fact, although good taste and elegance were cultivated under the pharaohs of Egypt, fashion didn't change at all. Ancient Egyptian jewelry and accessories of gold and precious stones indicate how extravagantly some people dressed, with highly stylized bracelets, necklaces, earrings, hair ornaments, headdresses, and even makeup all indicating to which class of the aristocracy or civil service an individual belonged. Egyptian women, who were relatively free from male domination, wore either the finest linen, which was almost transparent, or very little clothing at all. Wool was considered impure and never used, perhaps also because it was not needed in such a warm climate.

Although Cretan women followed Egyptian fashions, preclassical Greek women dressed modestly in the *chiton,* a beautiful long tunic of light wool which was elegantly draped and often weighted with lead at the hem so that it would hang gracefully. Although some dared to lighten their hair with lye or herbs, almost all Greek women tied their hair, wore little makeup, and used only light perfumes, in keeping with their reputation for modesty. However, over the centuries even Greek women began to wear fine cloth, bright colors, heels, necklaces, and scented ointments. In fact, the *peplos,* a shawllike garment worn by women, became so ornate that certain philosophers expressed disapproval—not that the men didn't dress just as elaborately.

Greek clothing

Women wearing chiton with peplos

The himation, or cloak

Man's chiton

The chiton worn by Greek men was a single long rectangle of cloth wound around the body and folded back over one shoulder. The men wore leather sandals and usually went bareheaded; they did, however, wear broad-brimmed hats for travel or special occasions. Each year Athenian girls wove a peplos, which they carried in a ritual procession to the temple of the goddess Athena as a gift on her feast day.

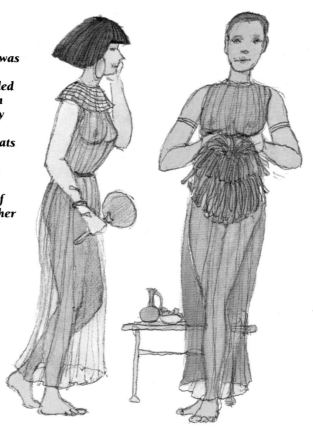

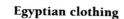

Egyptian clothing

The *nemeth*, the Egyptian man's headdress

A sandal worn by all social classes

Egyptian men wore a simple knee-length loincloth made of fine linen for the rich, and animal hide or coarse woven fiber for the poor. Egyptian dignitaries never appeared in public with bare heads, and although the normal headgear was a cloth which hung to the shoulders, all kinds of wigs and symbolic forms of headdress were also worn.

Typical plaited hairstyle adorned with jewels

19

Among the simplest and oldest forms of transportation were riding on an animal and being pulled on a sledge behind a beast of burden. Heavy weights like the blocks of stone used in the Egyptian pyramids were moved for centuries by means of wooden rollers, ancestors of the wheel. Funeral carriages pulled by wild donkeys some time around 3000 B.C. in Mesopotamia were the first wheeled carts. It is believed that the Scythians of the Asian steppes domesticated horses at a later date.

Transportation by water was easier than on land. Rafts were floated on hide sacks pumped full of air, while actual boats made of animal hides, but with wooden decks, sailed the rivers of Mesopotamia. On the calm waters of the Nile, the Egyptians were able to use boats made of bundles of papyrus, although for sea travel their vessels were made of wood.

The greatest sailors in antiquity were the Phoenicians, who set out from their invincible cities to establish trading centers all over the Mediterranean, founding colonies in Africa, Sicily, Sardinia, and the Iberian peninsula. Although little is known about Phoenician ships except that they first used anchors around 1000 B.C., Phoenician coins have been found as far from the Mediterranean as the Azores, in the middle of the Atlantic, indicating the great distances these people traveled.

An essential feature of the Greek *galley* was the keel, which stabilized the boat lengthwise, allowing the Greeks to cross the open sea rather than just hug the coastline. Merchant galleys had a single mast with a square sail, while war galleys, a miniature castle always at their prow, had two, and sometimes three, tiers of rowers.

The Persians built a royal road across their entire empire, from Sardis in Asia Minor, close to the Aegean shore, to Susa, beyond Babylon. The best means of transportation was by horse, although mules and camels were also used. Like the

Egyptians, the Persians had an efficient postal service, with posting stations located about every fifteen miles so that a hard-riding courier could cover up to ninety miles a day.

A Greek galley

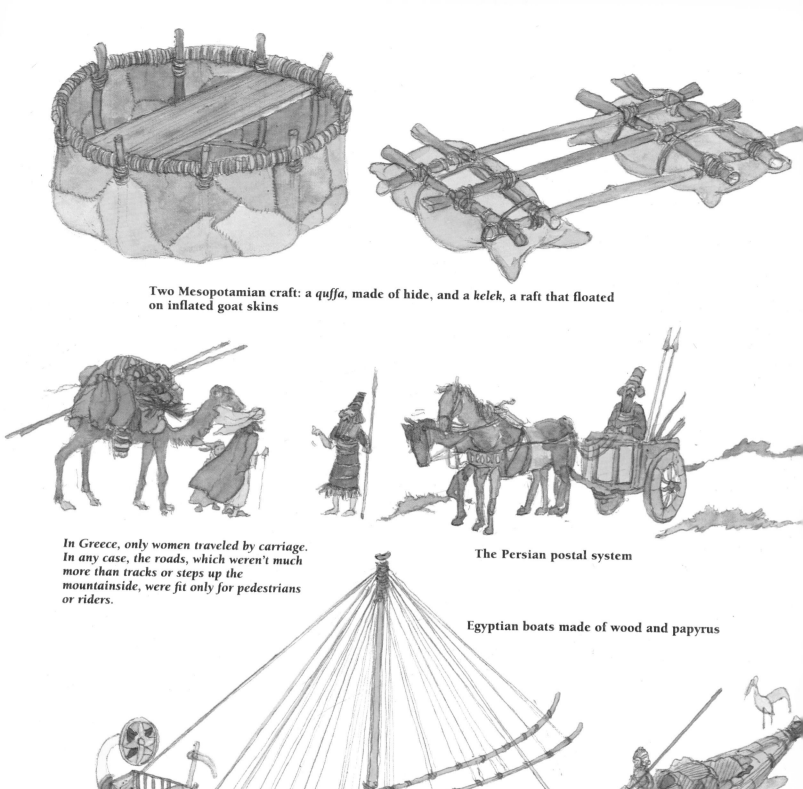

Two Mesopotamian craft: a *quffa*, made of hide, and a *kelek*, a raft that floated on inflated goat skins

In Greece, only women traveled by carriage. In any case, the roads, which weren't much more than tracks or steps up the mountainside, were fit only for pedestrians or riders.

The Persian postal system

Egyptian boats made of wood and papyrus

The primitive life of the Stone Age changed only when metal came into use for making stronger and more durable tools for work and hunting. Because the extraction and melting down of metals were among the greatest discoveries of antiquity, the various periods of prehistory are named accordingly—the Copper, Bronze, and Iron Ages. It is still not known how primitive man achieved the high temperatures necessary for melting metal, or how he was able to produce the precise and delicate craftsmanship archaeologists have found in his work.

In addition to the mastering of metalwork, several key innovations helped stimulate the progress of Western civilization.

In the mines, rock was shattered by means of sudden, extreme changes of temperature; first the rock was heated with fire and then cold water was poured on it. Thus fire and water were "domesticated," in one of man's earliest technological breakthroughs. The arch, used extensively in Roman times, was a revolutionary architectural invention. The wheel, which has a long history, was originally a solid circle of wood, made lighter for war chariots by means of hoops and spokes. Simple tools such as the lever, the pulley, the compass, and locking devices that used keys made an enormous difference in everyday life.

Certainly writing is one of the most important inventions of all time. In the fourth milennium B.C., the Sumerians already had a system of pictograms which gradually evolved into cuneiform writing. This involved inscribing tablets with a stylus then baking the clay to preserve the writing. The entire Sumerian language was represented by seven wedge shapes used in different combinations.

Egyptian hieroglyphic writing hardly changed over thousands of years. Although it might seem that each little figure represented the corresponding object, it actually represented a sound. Because there were no vowels, additional figures were added when necessary to clarify the meaning.

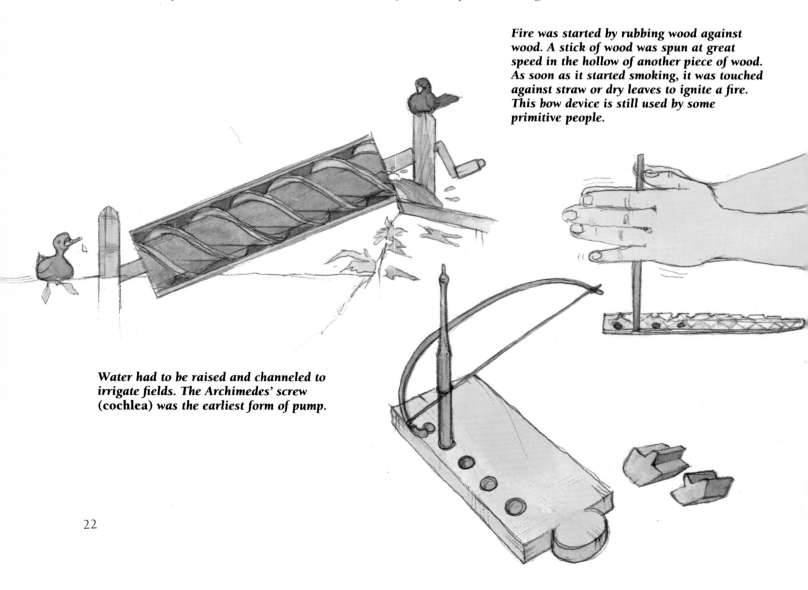

Fire was started by rubbing wood against wood. A stick of wood was spun at great speed in the hollow of another piece of wood. As soon as it started smoking, it was touched against straw or dry leaves to ignite a fire. This bow device is still used by some primitive people.

Water had to be raised and channeled to irrigate fields. The Archimedes' screw (cochlea) was the earliest form of pump.

The Greek mathematician and inventor Hero noticed how gas expands when heated and conceived of transforming heat into mechanical energy. At the time his insight was used only to open and close temple doors automatically, but the principle would later be applied to create engines, like the one that moves a car.

Egyptian hieroglyphics appeared on papyrus, as well as on mural inscriptions or carved in stone. Certain masons specialized in this type of decoration.

The evolution of cuneiform writing
Pictograms:

= **HEAD**

		Babylonian (1700 B.C.)	Neo-Assyrian (700 B.C.)	Neo-Babylonian (600 B.C.)

= **OX**

		Sumerian (2400 B.C.)		Akkadian (2200 B.C.)	Assyrian (1700 B.C.)		Neo-Assyrian (700 B.C.)	Neo-Babylonian (600 B.C.)

Most of the soldiers who fought for the great empires were slaves trained to use weapons and kept physically fit to endure the exhaustion of long marches and the hardships of war. Battles, however, were won on the basis of not only physical strength but successful tactics as well. The cream of the aristocracy directed the armies, with the most important campaigns being led by the ruler himself, accompanied by his war council.

In the second millennium B.C., Hittites, Egyptians, Assyrians, and Babylonians fought constantly for control of the trade crossroads in the area of Syria, which was also part of the invasion route for the peoples of the Asian steppes.

With the rise of more western powers, first in Greece and then in Italy, the great and abiding conflict between East and West began.

In the Greek city-state, the real soldier was the free man who could supply his own armor and weapons, called *panoplia*. In Sparta, which was the military state par excellence, soldiers lived in barracks until they were thirty, when they were allowed to marry. Married or not, they continued their military service until they were sixty.

Alexander of Macedon, who conquered all the civilized empires and pushed east as far as the Indus River, led the greatest army ever known, before the rise of the Roman Empire.

An Egyptian warrior and an Assyrian archer

The first ruler to create a vast empire in Mesopotamia was Sargon, whose bronze helmet is shown here.

The most famous Greek heroes were the Achaeans, who destroyed Troy around 1250 B.C. Achilles, Diomedes, Ajax, and Ulysses, as well as the Trojans Hector and Aeneas, live on in the great epics of Homer.

Military formation by phalanxes employed the use of shields, held side by side, forming a protective wall, while spears thrust forward repulsed the enemy. The first attack by bows and arrows and slings was made from a distance, with the cavalry following to break up the enemy lines so that the infantry could then engage in hand-to-hand combat.

A Macedonian warrior carrying a long lance

In the middle of the second millennium B.C., similarly built war chariots appeared almost simultaneously in all the great empires. Their speed and strength made them instruments of terror everywhere. The charioteer held the horses and kept the chariot on an even course, freeing the soldier behind him to throw his javelins and shoot his arrows.

One Great Empire Alone

Rome began as a small republic, no different from Etruscan city-states and Greek colonies in Italy. Its head magistrates were two consuls elected by the senate, a body of men representing the *patrician,* or aristocratic, class. The *plebeians,* or common people, had their own magistrates, known as *tribunes,* who looked after their interests.

However, after Rome conquered all the lands that bordered the Mediterranean, civil war broke out between the leading officers of the army. This struggle resulted in the concentration of power in the hands of one person, the emperor, who held his position for life.

The Roman Empire was at its greatest size around A.D. 100, when it stretched from Britain to Africa, and from Spain to Syria. It was at this time that the emperor Hadrian decided to forgo more conquest and concentrate on the administration of his vast empire. In making decisions, the en peror consulted the senate, which still represented the upper aristocracy and had retained at least some of its formal power.

Roman women played an important role in court intrigues and palace plots. Some were educated, but for the most part the "ideal woman" was a faithful wife and devoted mother who ran her huge household efficiently.

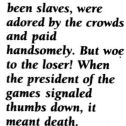

Although poets and artists were greatly honored and often enjoyed special privileges, the Romans loved the theater and the circus above all. Comedies especially revolved around *complicated plots. Because boxing, wrestling, fights between men and beasts, and chariot racing were all popular, famous actors and gladiators, even if they had originally* *been slaves, were adored by the crowds and paid handsomely. But woe to the loser! When the president of the games signaled thumbs down, it meant death.*

The Romans, being realists, understood that authority was not of divine origin, but was based on military strength and supported by popular consensus. Roman citizenship was gradually extended to all free men in the empire and even slaves could become free citizens *(liberti)*, either through the generosity of their owners or by paying a large ransom. Nevertheless, the great majority of the poor, as well as conquered subjects of other states, remained slaves, forced to work in the fields under masters who held the power of life and death over them. Slave revolts occurred from time to time, one of the most famous being that led by Spartacus. But the penalty for such action consisted of being nailed to a tree, covered with pitch, and burned to death.

Like soldiers and magistrates, patricians were for the most part landowners, while the slaves, aside from those who were miners, craftsmen, or galley oarsmen, worked in the fields. After all, the wealth of the empire depended on its agriculture.

The typical Roman patrician's house, whether in town or in the country, was a villa. It was a large structure with an interior square courtyard with porticoes and balconies, and it accommodated the household slaves as well as the family.

In the country villa there were storehouses and space for carts and tools. If the *pater familias,* the male head of the household, was a tradesman, the town villa contained shops and workshops on the ground floor, with living space on top. If the owner was a financier, professional man, politician, soldier, or literary man of leisure, the villa had grand suites of rooms. Public quarters were for outsiders who came and went, while private quarters for the family included bedrooms, a kitchen, a pantry, service rooms, and a *triclinium,* where meals were eaten while the diners reclined on couches. The degree of luxury depended on the owner's wealth, although the true

Roman, who tended to avoid extravagance, preferred standard conveniences such as heating and baths.

Ordinary townspeople lived in *insulae,* huge residential blocks several floors high which were bounded on all four sides by streets. The ground floor was lined with shops and workshops which often spilled out into the teeming, bustling streets. The magistrates who were in charge of housing and water made sure that the residences were well maintained and clean. With its eleven aqueducts, Rome probably had the best water supply of any ancient city and around A.D. 100 it could also boast of a good sewage system and 144 public lavatories.

Cities and towns founded or redesigned by the Romans followed an orderly plan of axial streets. The central square, or *forum,* with its temple and *basilica* was located where the two main streets met. The right-angled layout of streets can be seen in many cities today.

The one-family house of the artisan, tradesman, or small independent farmer remained virtually unchanged for centuries. The workshop and shop, or barn and shed for farm equipment, were on the ground floor, with two rooms above, one for the daytime and the other for night. Both water and fire were kept outside the living area. Houses had a small brick oven inside, braziers to provide heat, and oil lamps for lighting.

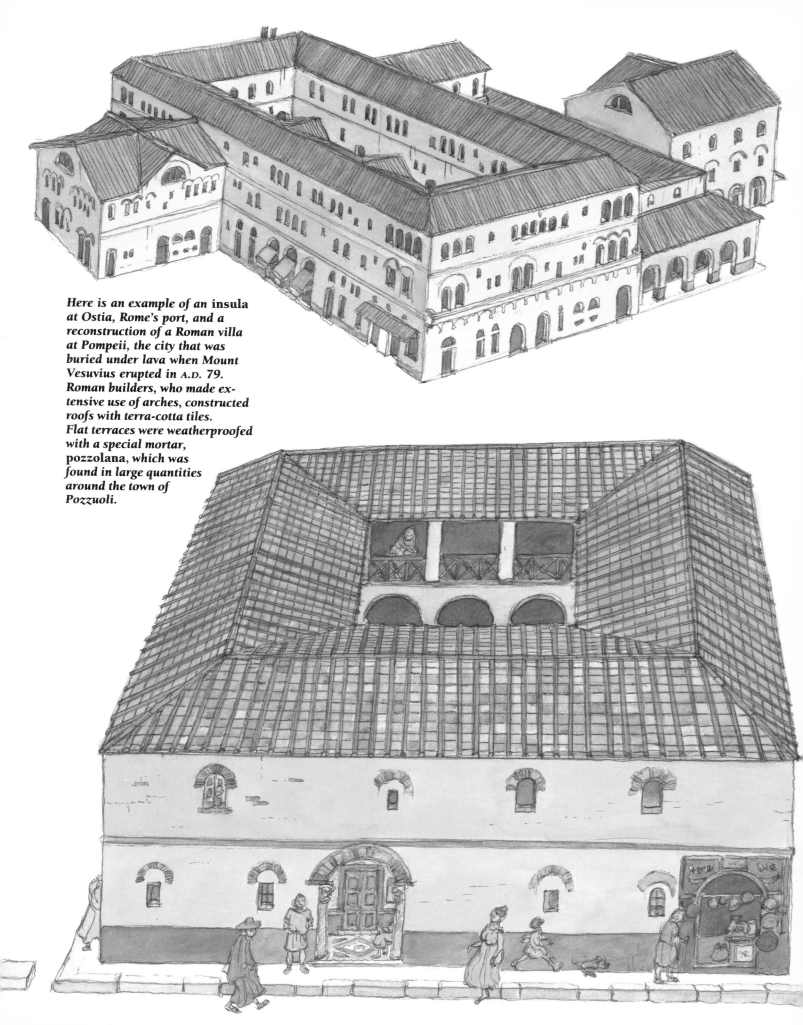

Here is an example of an insula at Ostia, Rome's port, and a reconstruction of a Roman villa at Pompeii, the city that was buried under lava when Mount Vesuvius erupted in A.D. 79. Roman builders, who made extensive use of arches, constructed roofs with terra-cotta tiles. Flat terraces were weatherproofed with a special mortar, pozzolana, which was found in large quantities around the town of Pozzuoli.

There were two types of Roman farms: the family business run by the *pater familias* and his wife, children, and servants; and the large estate worked by slaves. With little manpower at his disposal, the small farmer wasn't able to spend time studying or trying out new tools that might have increased his productivity and lightened his work load. His aim was not to sell vast quantities of produce, but simply to support his family and make them as comfortable as possible. Consequently, he raised crops that varied from cereals to vegetables and fruit, and cultivated grapevines for wine, olive trees for olive oil, and woodland for timber.

Once their campaigns were over, soldiers of the empire received farmland as a reward for their services. When it was possible, they chose the most fertile areas, with either springs or rivers available for irrigation. Great stretches of marshland were also reclaimed, among them the Po Valley in Italy, the mouth of the Rhone River in southern France, and the land around Cambridge, England. This reclamation not only made more land available for farming, but also lessened the occurrence of diseases such as malaria.

Large estates farmed by great numbers of slaves produced mostly cereal crops, wheat, barley, and oats. Unfortunately, the continuous export of slaves drained manpower from such areas as the African provinces that had once been highly productive.

Agriculture necessitated careful land management, including, for example, the right ratio of workers to tillable land. The Romans were expert at dividing the land evenly into suitable farm sizes. They used an instrument called a groma to mark out the right-angled corners of farmland. Because the soil was double-plowed crosswise, the fields were square.

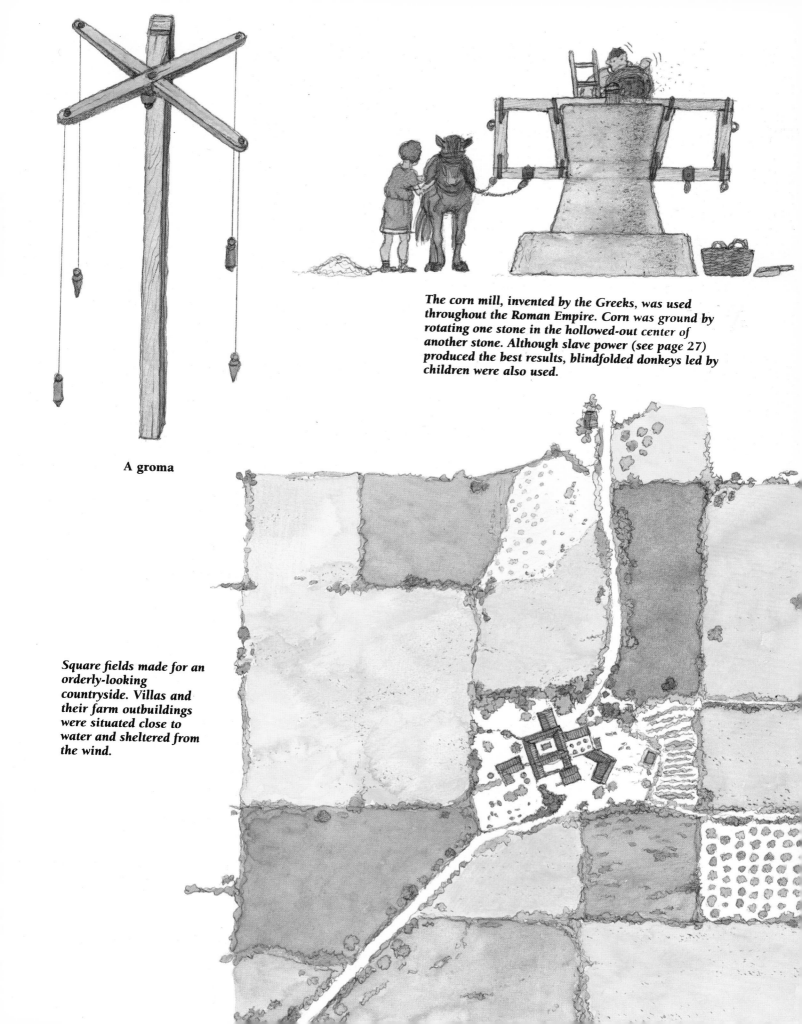

The corn mill, invented by the Greeks, was used throughout the Roman Empire. Corn was ground by rotating one stone in the hollowed-out center of another stone. Although slave power (see page 27) produced the best results, blindfolded donkeys led by children were also used.

A groma

Square fields made for an orderly-looking countryside. Villas and their farm outbuildings were situated close to water and sheltered from the wind.

The Romans' extensive construction programs required many highly skilled architects and craftsmen. As a building rose, stone blocks were raised up inclines that were erected higher and higher until the building was finished and the inclines could be removed. Teams of men with strong ropes hoisted columns and obelisks into place, and precise calculations guaranteed that each piece would be moved into exactly the right position. Sometimes pulleys were attached to a wheel that was turned by men walking inside it.

Using the same principle with water power, the Romans invented the water mill, which produced flour on an "industrial" scale. These mills were confined mainly to the center of the empire, however, with the old man-ually powered mills used elsewhere. Often the mill and the oven were in the same building, which meant that grain would go in and bread would come out.

In a city like Rome, which had over a million inhabitants, there was a thriving clothing trade, with many goods imported from the provinces. The East was the best source of luxury items such as fine woven and dyed materials, jewelry, and perfume. The Romans always admired the Greeks for their artistic traditions, and in the second century B.C., the emperor Hadrian summoned all the best Greek artists to come to Rome to revive Greek styles. Egyptian obelisks were brought to Rome to beautify the city; in fact, most of the ancient obelisks that have survived to this day are found in Rome.

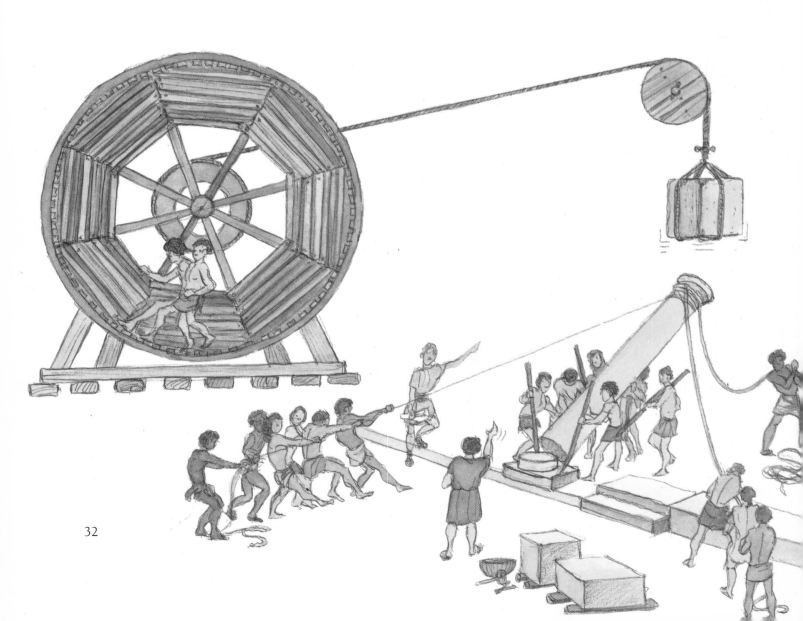

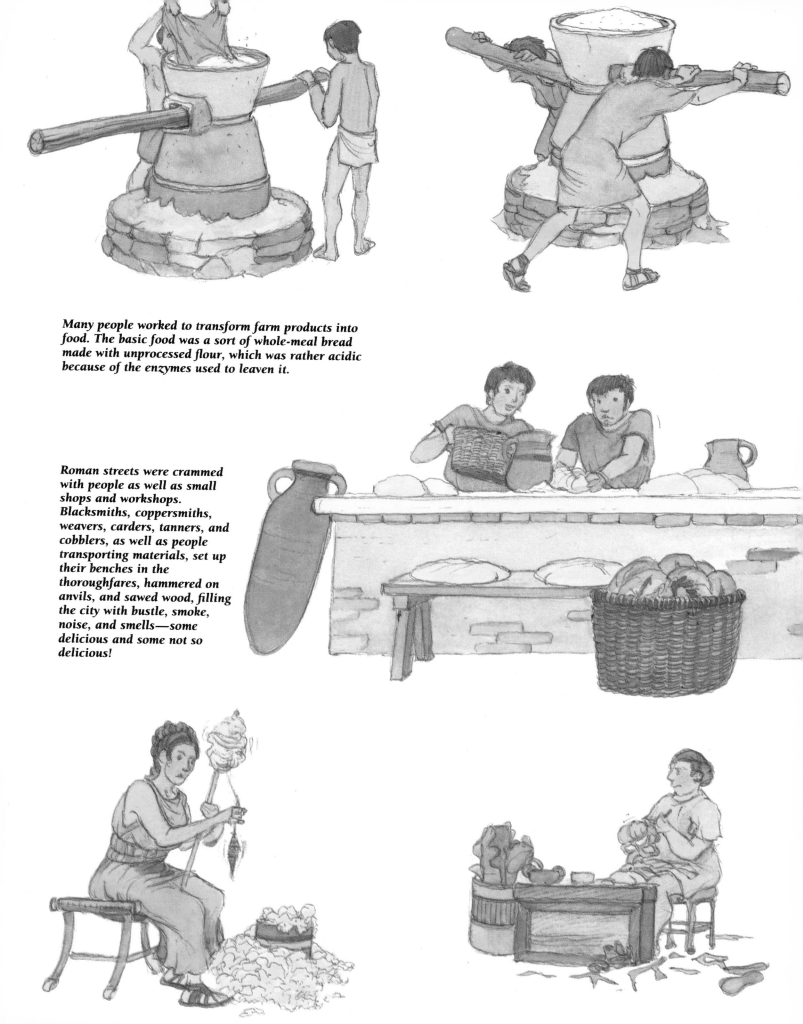

Many people worked to transform farm products into food. The basic food was a sort of whole-meal bread made with unprocessed flour, which was rather acidic because of the enzymes used to leaven it.

Roman streets were crammed with people as well as small shops and workshops. Blacksmiths, coppersmiths, weavers, carders, tanners, and cobblers, as well as people transporting materials, set up their benches in the thoroughfares, hammered on anvils, and sawed wood, filling the city with bustle, smoke, noise, and smells—some delicious and some not so delicious!

At the height of the empire, Rome alone consumed virtually all the tribute paid by Sicily, Egypt, and the African provinces, not to mention huge quantities of grain and oil which were imported by private merchants from Spain.

The large cities served as both administrative centers and trading posts for merchandise that traveled to and from Rome along the empire's vast network of roads and waterways. Even in the most distant provinces, the Roman life-style, with its desire for luxury goods, was imitated. Consequently, transportation of goods was essential in this world of intense international trade. Contributing to the ease with which merchandise could be moved were minimal customs barriers, a single currency, well-maintained roads and ports, and the almost complete eradication of piracy.

Nevertheless, Rome, with its free market and thousands of small traders, never introduced a unified trading system to concentrate its capital. Goods were distributed through small-scale outlets, with dealers specializing in one type of product so that merchandise—such as incense and wild beasts from Ethiopia, the latter for use in the circuses, spices from India, and silk from China—often traveled hundreds of miles and passed through many hands only to end up in some tiny shop in Rome.

The major Mediterranean port was Alexandria, with a population of half a million. The great caravan routes, protected by border towns such as Palmyra and Petra, led eastward from the Syrian coastal ports, and from Antioch to Gaza. With Roman authorization, Greek, Phoenician, and Arabian merchants journeyed all around the Mediterranean and down the Red Sea into the Persian Gulf. Roman coins have even been found as far away as southern India.

Apart from grain crises in Roman colonies in Greece, the provinces were self-sufficient as far as food and everyday goods. Trade involved primarily luxury items such as fine pottery, skillfully worked glass, jewelry, ointments, cloth, carpets, and works of art. Papyrus was used throughout the Mediterranean world for writing.

Tonsor, the barber

Lanius, the butcher

Vinarius, the wine merchant

Pomarius, the greengrocer

The finest of the world's goods could be found in Rome, where distribution was handled through a network of specialized shops.

Caupo, the innkeeper

The *tunic,* originally sleeveless, was a basic Roman garment; it was worn only by Roman citizens after they had come of age. For warmth some men, such as the emperor Augustus, simply wore more than one. Although the tunic, which was pulled on over the head, was normally knee-length, some dandies wore it longer; later it was worn ankle-length. Adult males wore belts only outdoors, not indoors. The *toga* was a garment which was pulled on over the tunic and wrapped around the body, with the different types of togas denoting the wearer's social position or rank: priests and magistrates wore a *toga praetexta* with a vertical purple band in front; the all-white *toga candida,* worn without a tunic in order to display war wounds proudly, identified candidates for the civil service and public positions. There were various styles of sandals, some laced around the feet and others strapped up the calf of the leg.

Over their *stola,* a tunic of sorts which tied at the sides and under the breasts, women wore a *palla,* a wide mantle which passed under the right arm and hung over the left shoulder to the ground. Women's footwear included the *soccus,* a comfortable slipper.

Jeweled gold brooches kept clothes and hair in place. Rings glittered on every finger except the middle one, for magical reasons, while engaged couples exchanged gold-plated iron rings that were worn on the left-hand ring finger, believed to be connected by a nerve to the heart.

The *lacerna*, a heavy cloak

Like the Greeks, the
Romans wore hats only for
traveling.
When young men donned
the adult toga, they kept
their arms wrapped up for
a year, as a token of
humility.

Women's fashions changed often, and
Roman women, who loved fine
materials, bright colors, and rich
embroidery glittering with gold thread,
wore elaborate clothing. The bridal
tunic, which was white, was woven in a
single length by a weaver standing up.

The *carbatina*, a popular sandal

Because the earliest Romans were mostly shepherds living in the hills of Latium, they knew little about the sea. It is believed that a Carthaginian ship that wrecked on Latin shores was the original model for Roman ships. In any event, in time, the Romans, using the most sophisticated nautical technology of the period, built a navy that was unsurpassed for over a thousand years.

Once the Mediterranean was conquered and purged of pirates, a merchant fleet was developed to bring goods to Rome from the provinces. In order to increase safety, especially in storms, these trading vessels, *onerariae,* were redesigned and improved. The hulls were more solid and curved; the stern was taller and broader to allow for a larger sail to catch favorable winds. The massive main mast consisted of several shafts lashed together tightly; a foresail insured maneuverability at the bow, while two additional triangular topsails were hoisted above the square sail between the mast and the two yardarms. Many ships had deck cabins for the sailors, while a gallery on the poop deck held a shrine to the patron deity.

The Roman road system was equally well developed. From around A.D. 100 to 150, the road network stretched uninterrupted, except for necessary sea passages, from Hadrian's Wall in northern *Britannia,* or Roman Britain, to the edge of the Sahara, and from the Straits of Gibraltar to the Persian Gulf. These roads were built and paved in three layers; a foundation of stone blocks was covered with packed rubble hardened with mortar, which in turn was topped with paving stones. Europe wouldn't see a road network of such quality for a thousand years or more. Of special importance were the passes over the Alps which, ironically, were used by the invaders who eventually conquered Rome.

Roman warships were built for attack rather than for strategic maneuvering. Enemy warships were rammed and then boarded across a special gangway bridge, or corvus, which was thrown out from the Roman bow onto the enemy ship, linking the two vessels together.

The earliest examples of on-ship storage were large terra-cotta containers built into the ship. These were suitable for carrying oil, grain or wine.

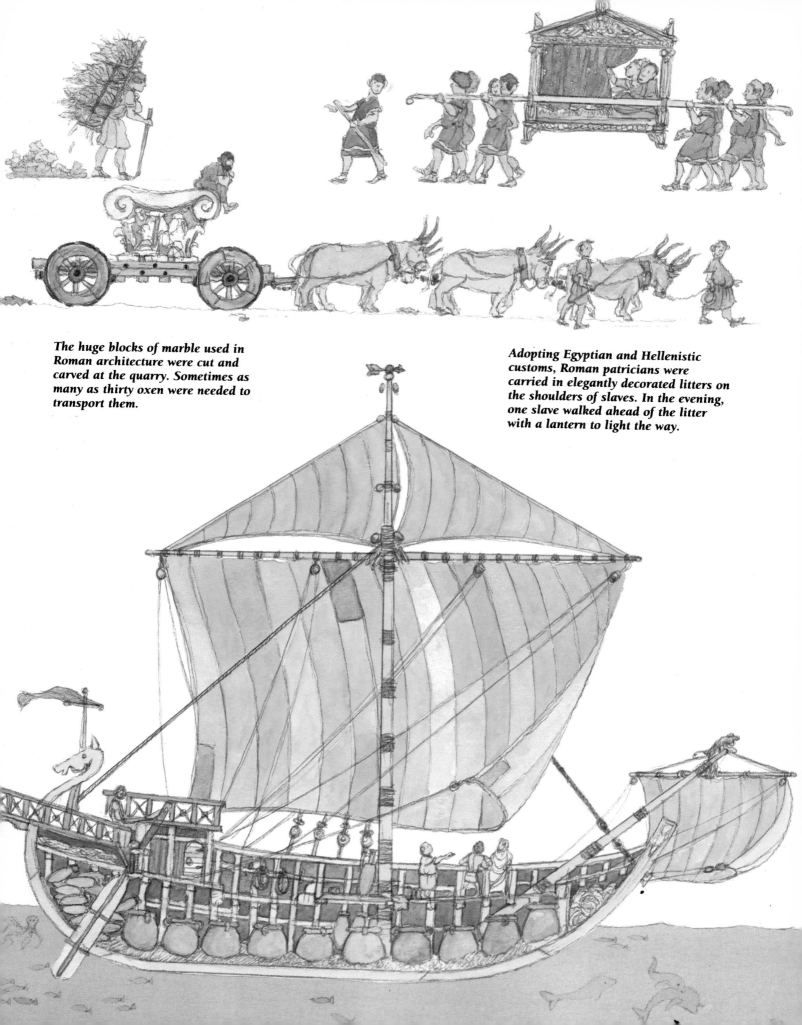

The huge blocks of marble used in Roman architecture were cut and carved at the quarry. Sometimes as many as thirty oxen were needed to transport them.

Adopting Egyptian and Hellenistic customs, Roman patricians were carried in elegantly decorated litters on the shoulders of slaves. In the evening, one slave walked ahead of the litter with a lantern to light the way.

The clearest evidence today of Roman occupation of an area is in the buildings left behind. As builders, the Romans surpassed all earlier civilizations, laying down three basic laws of architecture: *firmitas,* solidity; *utilitas,* the purpose of any particular building and the functional handling of space; and *venustas,* order and beauty. Arches, which had been used experimentally by the Etruscans, were developed and perfected so that it was possible to have large empty spaces between supporting pillars without needing perishable wooden beams or stone lintels, which were bulky and awkward to position and fragile under heavy loads. Light, elegant buildings with galleries of arches were not only easy to build because they were constructed with small dressed stones or bricks, but also economical because they required less load-bearing structure.

The Romans were the first to use water for mechanical power. Rivers turned paddle wheels connected to shafts, thus harnessing power. The result? The original water mill.

Adequate drinking water was a constant source of concern for Roman administrators. The solution was to supply water from wells or springs, sometimes many miles from the city, along aqueducts; these consisted of channels, lead piping, and syphons supported by bridges of slender tiered arcades. Around A.D. 100, Rome had nine aqueducts, eventually increased to as many as nineteen.

Although the Roman Empire was always interested in finding new lands to conquer, the sheer vastness of the territory that had to be governed, combined with its almost unlimited supply of low-cost labor, meant there was little incentive to seek new resources or to advance technology. However, this was certainly not the case for either the government or the army, the two spheres of influence in which Roman genius expressed itself most fully. All later Western legal systems have been based on Roman legislation.

In Rome water was distributed by small pipes. Around A.D. 200, there were eleven public baths and over 800 private ones, while 1,300 public fountains and cisterns provided many gallons of water daily for every inhabitant. Patrician villas developed a hot-water heating system, complete with an outside boiler to heat the water, which then flowed under the floors, warming them. Even ships had plumbing systems.

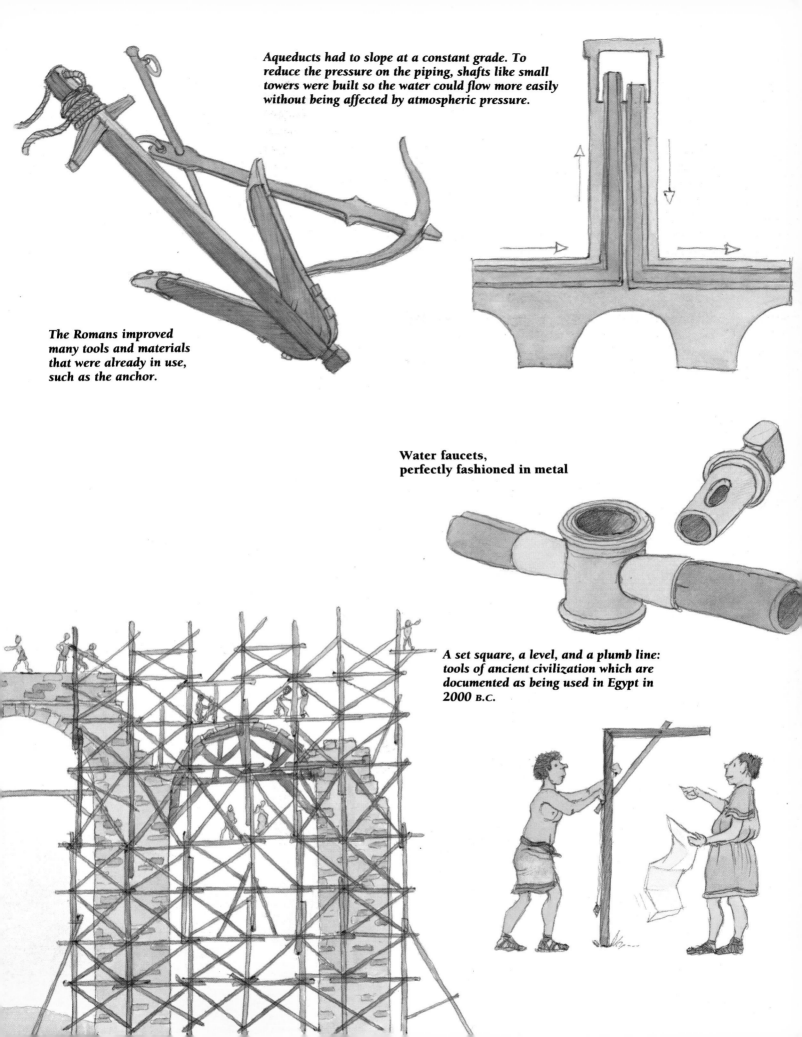

Aqueducts had to slope at a constant grade. To reduce the pressure on the piping, shafts like small towers were built so the water could flow more easily without being affected by atmospheric pressure.

The Romans improved many tools and materials that were already in use, such as the anchor.

Water faucets, perfectly fashioned in metal

A set square, a level, and a plumb line: tools of ancient civilization which are documented as being used in Egypt in 2000 B.C.

Under the Roman Republic, the army was made up of those free citizens who could afford to equip and arm themselves and who had interests and land to defend. However, with the young men absent on long campaigns, farmwork suffered. Two solutions were possible: like the Spartans, the Romans could subjugate other peoples and force them to do the work, or they could organize a professional army.

Any male Roman citizen, no matter how poor he was or where he came from, could enter the *legions*. Armed and supported by the state, these soldiers, who were fiercely loyal to their generals as well as to Rome, threw themselves into adventure and conquest, at the same time enhancing their own personal prestige. Rivalry between generals attempting to seize power in Rome provoked bloody civil wars. After the death of Julius Caesar, the true founder of the empire although he never took the title of emperor, many successful warlords were hailed as emperor by their legions and were kept on the throne by their armies. The history of Rome is the history of an empire racked by ambition and violence.

The Roman army was able to conquer such a vast empire because of its fine equipment and training, its perfectly organized ranks, and above all, its strict discipline. But it must be remembered that if the prizes were rich, the punishments were harsh.

"Barbarians" from the north

A standardbearer

A legionnaire with his pack

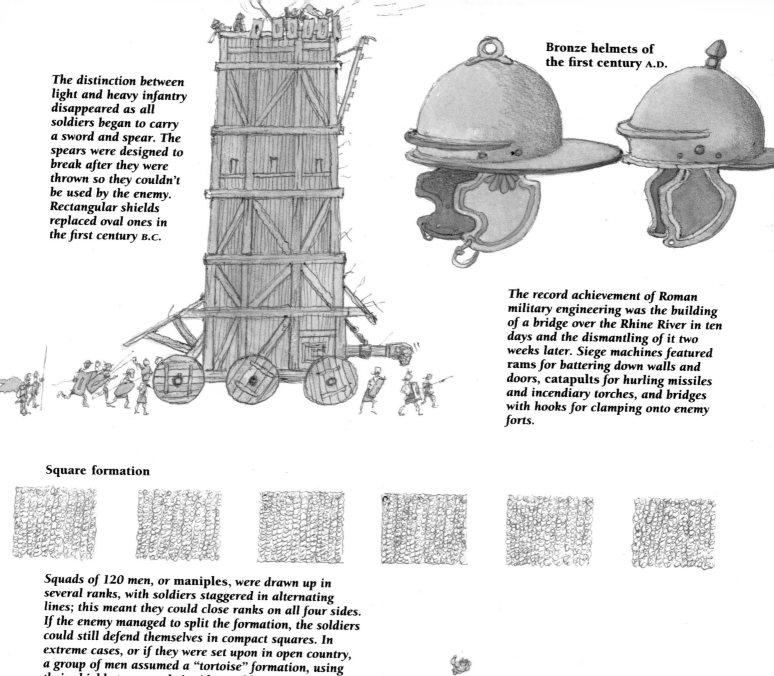

The distinction between light and heavy infantry disappeared as all soldiers began to carry a sword and spear. The spears were designed to break after they were thrown so they couldn't be used by the enemy. Rectangular shields replaced oval ones in the first century B.C.

Bronze helmets of the first century A.D.

The record achievement of Roman military engineering was the building of a bridge over the Rhine River in ten days and the dismantling of it two weeks later. Siege machines featured rams for battering down walls and doors, catapults for hurling missiles and incendiary torches, and bridges with hooks for clamping onto enemy forts.

Square formation

Squads of 120 men, or maniples, were drawn up in several ranks, with soldiers staggered in alternating lines; this meant they could close ranks on all four sides. If the enemy managed to split the formation, the soldiers could still defend themselves in compact squares. In extreme cases, or if they were set upon in open country, a group of men assumed a "tortoise" formation, using their shields to cover their sides and heads, thus enabling them to withstand even a chariot attack.

Before the Year 1000

Although the Romans had set up well-fortified lines of defense along the Rhine and the Danube, hordes of Huns from the eastern European steppes invaded from the north, changing the political map of the Western Roman Empire within a matter of decades. These primitive, warlike tribes, with their great migrations of a strong and vigorous people, thirsted for conquest.

After the Roman legions were gone, the struggle for supreme power and for a reunited and reorganized empire continued among the different ethnic groups of invaders under their various leaders and kings. First the Franks, then the Saxons, and later the Swabians sought control of the empire, now called the Holy Roman Empire because it was recognized by the Church and its emperors were crowned by the pope.

The new system of social organization known as feudalism was based on the fief, or feud, an area administered by a feudal lord delegated by the emperor. This feudal lord, in turn, had others under him, right down to the lowest vassal. Once fiefs became hereditary, a new aristocracy was born and a nobility emerged. The center of the feud was the lord's castle; peasant villages clustered around it so that when danger threatened, the

Emperor

Pope

Feudal lords

High clergy

Knights

The military class retained its importance; the imperial army had to assert the unity of the empire constantly, even when this meant using force internally. The army also had to halt the hordes of Vikings in the north, Magyars in the east, and Saracens in the south.

Two groups enjoyed certain freedoms: craftsmen, who began to organize themselves into companies and guilds, and the top officials of the Church hierarchy, who for a long time represented society's only stable authority.
The large numbers of farm laborers, the glebe serfs, were the lowest of the feudal social order.

Artisans

Low clergy

Serfs

44

peasants could flee inside the castle and defend it.

When destruction and plague resulted in a food crisis, there was a sharp drop in population. Eventually all people, whatever their social position, had to help rebuild society, with the Christian Church, which was now spreading throughout the West, acting as a moral spur. The Benedictine monasteries, with their disciplined and constructive life-style, contributed greatly by setting an example to the secular community.

The abbot, who was often a bishop, was elected by the chapter of assembled monks to be in charge of the monastery. Each monk had his own tasks of both work and prayer. The scribes, or amanuenses, had the vital job of copying the works of classical authors and the Church fathers, bringing together the cultural heritage of the Romans and the new culture of medieval Christendom from which the universities emerged.

Abbot

Members of the chapter

The various activities of the monastery

Scribes

The inhabitants of northern Europe, some of whom were still seminomadic and unfamiliar with city life, developed their own forms of collective dwellings that usually sheltered more than one family. Living in such a cold climate as theirs meant that fire, essential for survival, was the focal point of the house. Sloping roofs allowed rain and melted snow to drain off, while smoke from the fire escaped through a small hole at the top of the roof where the support poles met.

Framework building techniques, called half-timbering, were popular for centuries, partly because conifer trees were so readily available.

Villages, normally built around a central spring or well, were surrounded by a protective ditch which was often reinforced by a sturdy palisade. In addition to the human dwellings, there were also enclosures for the domestic animals, the most important of which were horses, used for work and transportation, and pigs, which provided meat for the winter. Although the nobles' castles had a similar layout, the walls and towers rested on solid stone foundations, while the roofs were occasionally metal-sheeted.

The towns founded by the Romans were more or less abandoned after the barbarian invasions and lay in ruins. The new centers of urban growth became the feudal castles and the monasteries, leaving the diocese and the office of bishop as the only elements of organization that the new society retained.

46

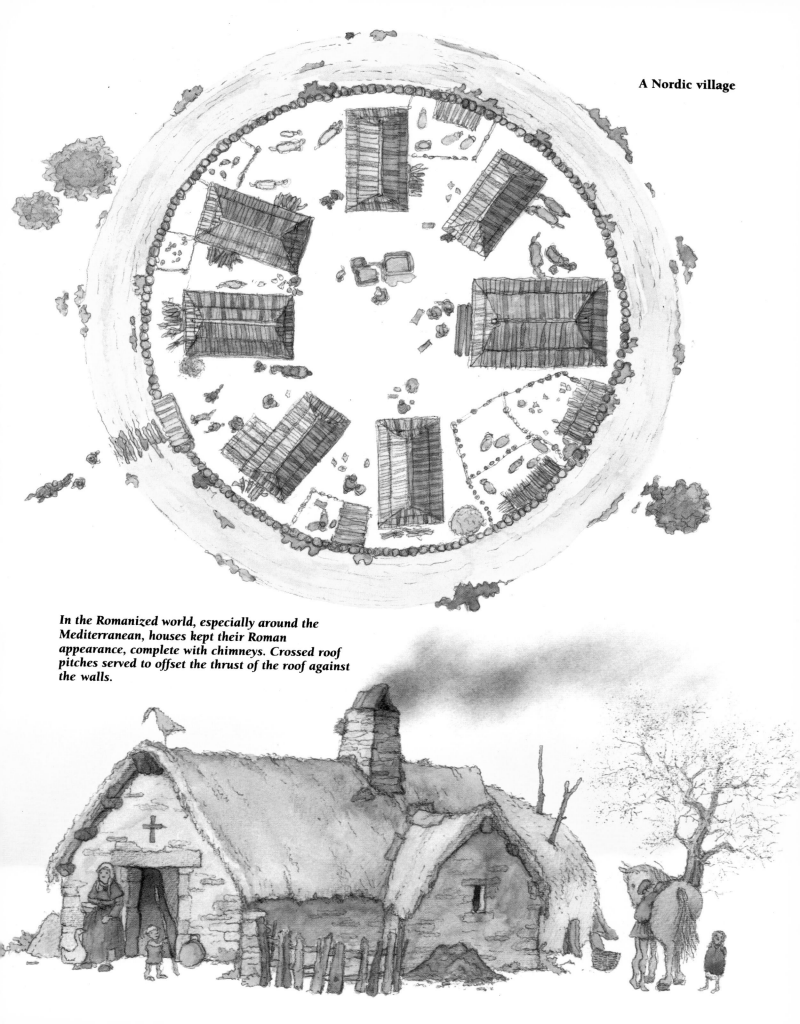

A Nordic village

In the Romanized world, especially around the Mediterranean, houses kept their Roman appearance, complete with chimneys. Crossed roof pitches served to offset the thrust of the roof against the walls.

The agricultural crisis, which was already underway when the Roman Empire was beginning to crumble, lasted for centuries and was accompanied by terrible plagues. The invasions uprooted whole peoples, greatly affecting society's relationship to the land. The Goths and Lombards settled in northern Italy (hence the name Lombardy); the Swabians and Vandals in Andalusia in southern Spain, and the Franks in Gaul (modern France).

Because systems of irrigation and land reclamation had fallen into disrepair, the land was soon devastated, and the arrival of new migrating tribes made the recovery period even longer and more difficult.

The Germanic kings divided their conquered territories into fiefs, putting a trusted follower in charge of each fief. Farmers belonged to the fief in which they worked and they were not allowed to leave. No longer a slave, the farmer was a serf of the glebe—that is, of the land—and he had to farm the lord's land in addition to producing food for himself. In exchange for *corvée,* the work they did without pay on the lord's land, peasants were given small plots of land to grow their own vegetables and were allowed to keep certain pasturing, hunting, and fishing rights. Although they could take wood from uncultivated areas of the feud, a certain amount of all they produced (known as *gratuities*) had to go to the castle.

Whatever the peasant farmer or shepherd managed to put aside for the winter was always at risk of being seized by bands of robbers or the marauding armies that constantly crossed Europe in search of power. Frequently the peasant farmer had to become a soldier and defend the castle in which he had the right to seek refuge.

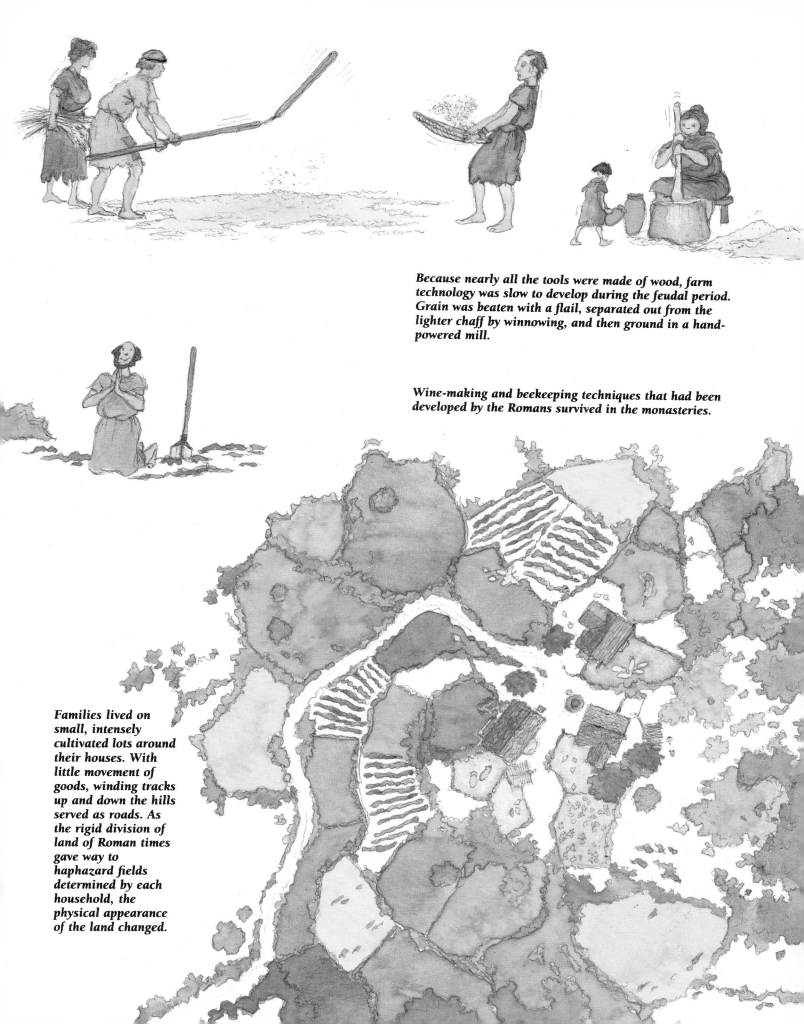

Because nearly all the tools were made of wood, farm technology was slow to develop during the feudal period. Grain was beaten with a flail, separated out from the lighter chaff by winnowing, and then ground in a hand-powered mill.

Wine-making and beekeeping techniques that had been developed by the Romans survived in the monasteries.

Families lived on small, intensely cultivated lots around their houses. With little movement of goods, winding tracks up and down the hills served as roads. As the rigid division of land of Roman times gave way to haphazard fields determined by each household, the physical appearance of the land changed.

The Germanic races, who had fewer slaves for man-power, were more interested than the Romans in developing tools that would make physical labor easier and more productive. Strong axes and saws were used for felling trees, while sharp sword blades were produced for war. With ferrous land common in central Europe, and with the use of coal-fueled forges equipped with bellows, great advances were made during this period in metalworking; iron production in particular increased greatly.

Nestling at the foot of the castle walls, the feudal village included a row of artisans' workshops—a blacksmith, who shod horses and made chains; a woodworker and carpenter, who served as cart maker and cooper too; a tanner, who worked the leather to make clothes and armor; and a weaver, to whom the women took the wool they had spun during long winter evenings by the fire.

Only in the large towns did artisans become independent craftsmen whose products were bought by the wealthy and even by kings. These skilled specialists were expert at gilding, creating copper and silver reliefs, sculpting marble and ivory, assembling intricate mosaics, and producing fine ironwork. Their style was a combination of Roman love of realism, Byzantine refinement of decoration, and the strength and simplicity of the barbarians.

Although writing survived in the castles, it flourished primarily in the monasteries. Illuminators, who were often illiterate themselves, spent long hours illuminating capital letters and filling entire pages with small, lavishly done illustrations. Because they frequently featured red lead, or *minium*, these pictures were called "miniatures." Kings, both at court and during their travels, were always accompanied by a scribe to whom they dictated letters and records of events.

When a piece of metal came red-hot out of the forge, the blacksmith gripped it with tongs and hammered it into shape on the anvil. As soon as he was satisfied with the shape, he tempered it by plunging it into water, where the sudden cooling gave the inner structure of the iron greater rigidity and strength. The forge and the casting furnace were made of heat-resistant metals and were blown constantly with bellows to obtain maximum heat from the burning wood or coal.

Here we see two illuminated capital Os.

Byzantine-style gold and pearl necklaces were a specialty of jewelers in Ravenna and Venice.

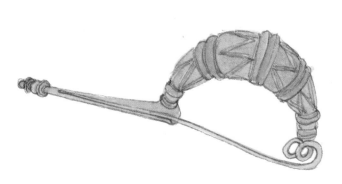

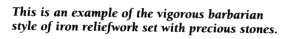

This ivory plaque engraved with the Flagellation of Christ shows great technical skill.

This is an example of the vigorous barbarian style of iron reliefwork set with precious stones.

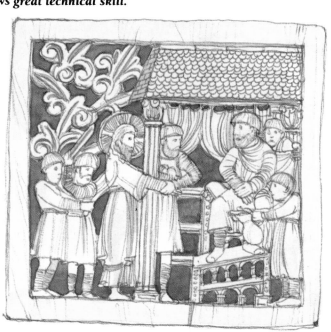

During those years trade suffered from the lack of production. Although there wasn't much excess farm produce available for sale, the depopulated towns didn't require great stores of provisions either. Farmers brought their goods into town, and each town set aside specific areas where produce from the countryside could be sold. Usually it was the old Roman forum that evolved into the town marketplace.

Along with other Roman achievements, the road system also fell into bad disrepair. Long journeys were always interrupted, and goods didn't travel much more than a couple of dozen miles a day. Traders had to cross different fiefdoms, each one imposing its own duties and tolls so that the cost of transportation from one town to another could be as much as fifty percent of the original price of the article being transported. The passes over the Alps had also fallen into disrepair, and trade routes between Italy and Germany had to travel down the Rhone Valley and the Ligurian coast, making the journey three times as long as a more direct route. Although sea transportation was less costly than land transportation, it was not always possible; when it was, the merchant had to entrust his wares to a third party—a risky business.

Communications were better in the Near East, where the Arab world was growing and the Byzantine Empire still flourished. Trade with the East, though not as strong as it had once been, was still vigorous, and from the exotic cities of Damascus, Mosul, and Baghdad came luxurious cloths named after their origins—damask, muslin and baldachin.

To avoid the confusion of different currencies, payment was often made in goods of equal worth. At the same time that Charlemagne in Europe was reforming the monetary system and imposing the use of silver only, the Arabs were introducing a new gold coin, the dinar, which was worth $\frac{1}{240}$ of a pound of gold.

Supplies of corn, stored in castle granaries, constituted the wealth of the feudal lords, used for bartering and for paying tribute to the sovereign.

Roman influences in clothing survived, although they were now enriched by the elaborate decorative styles of the East and the Byzantine world, as well as the more sober traditions of northern Europe, where thick, heavy woolen clothing was worn.

During this era breeches became a basic part of male dress, especially among the working classes. Leather breeches were cut tight around the legs, while cloth breeches were pulled tight with laces. A knee- or calf-length tunic or doublet, which was tucked up under the belt when its wearer was working, was worn over the breeches. In winter a cape was worn diagonally over the tunic, leaving the right arm free. Those who could afford them wore soft leather shoes laced at the front, while the less fortunate wore wooden clogs or went barefoot.

Women dressed in long, colorfully dyed tunics. The earth and vegetable dyes used were fixed with acidic substances such as urine or chicken dye. Women didn't cut their hair, but wore it long, often down to their thighs.

The use of two different colors in a person's clothing, usually yellow and blue or red and green, originated in the north. This fashion, which spread throughout medieval Europe, was adopted by town criers, standard-bearers, and soldiers.

Byzantine crowns, studded with pearls and precious stones, influenced the diadems of new Germanic aristocrats; although these were often made of iron, they were finished off with gold and jewels.

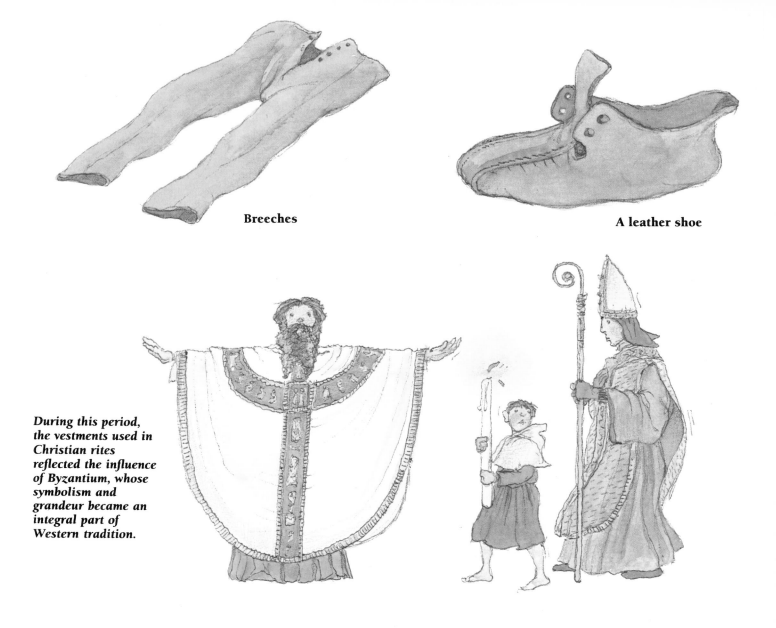

Breeches

A leather shoe

During this period, the vestments used in Christian rites reflected the influence of Byzantium, whose symbolism and grandeur became an integral part of Western tradition.

Clothes of various classes

Lady of the manor

Merchant

Peasant

Apprentice

Because the wheel saw little development under the Romans, ordinary wagons still used solid wheels, which exerted great friction on the axles. Although attempts were made to remedy this by covering the axles with leather and bronze, the real solution lay in two developments from northern Europe: lighter wheels with spokes, and bearings in the form of small wooden rollers between the axle and the hub. Iron rims, sometimes studded with nails for a better grip, lengthened the life of the wheel, but they did so much damage to streets that some towns forbade their use. Consequently, for town driving, leather rims were adopted.

Over the years the Roman roads deteriorated. Farmers removed the paving stones to use in the foundations of their buildings, leaving only an earth surface, which actually made traveling by horseback easier. To avoid paying tolls, riders tended to take roundabout routes, no matter how long and tortuous, so that gradually a new "road" network emerged that was far more irregular and uncoordinated than the precise, straight lines of the old Roman roads.

Meanwhile, the horse's harness was improved, with shafts replacing the single pole.

Shipbuilding continued in the tradition of the skilled axmen of the Baltic Sea and North Sea. Ships' hulls were made of overlapping planks fastened with iron pegs. As the design of ships improved and developed rapidly, the Irish, and then the Vikings from Scandinavia became superb navigators, as their ships were able to travel farther and farther from home. The Vikings, who buried their leaders in their ships, explored as far as Greenland and the northern shores of North America.

Deforestation increased the amount of land that could be farmed. Tree trunks were floated downriver to seaport shipyards.

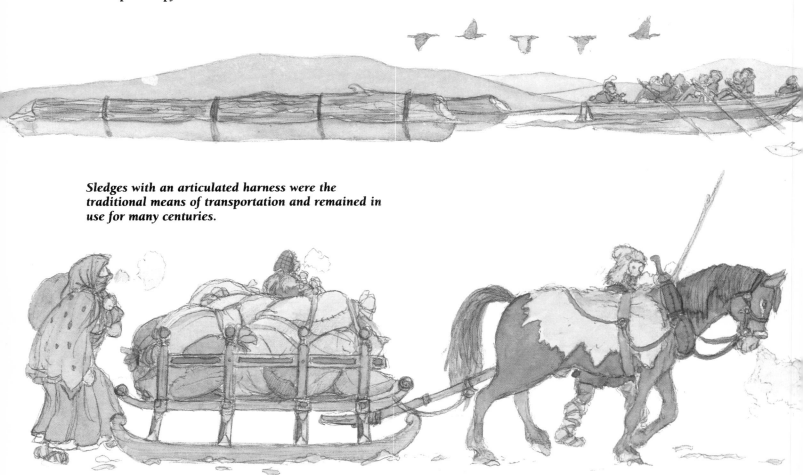

Sledges with an articulated harness were the traditional means of transportation and remained in use for many centuries.

The wheelbarrow, which is based on the lever
principle, was so efficient in increasing one person's
work capacity that it is still in common use today.

A Viking ship

As agriculture gradually recovered from its crisis state, the population increased, making the techniques of storing and preserving food ever more important. Although each area kept its old traditions, various new ways of making cheese and salting meat and fish became widespread. In order to sell their fish, the people of northern Europe gutted and cleaned them, then either packed them closely in barrels, like herring, or dried them, like cod. Preserving in oil or brine was more common in the south.

In the Germanic world, there were still no real towns, only villages, like Charlemagne's capital, Aquisgranum, known today as Aachen, which had only a few thousand inhabitants. However, as Germanic society became more urban, building techniques had to be acquired and developed. The master builders of northern Italy, who were summoned north to work with local masters, played a major role in this growth of cities.

The real builders of the age were the Arabs: they acquired Byzantine building skills and developed them further, in fanciful structures topped with domes. Córdoba, the capital of the Spanish caliphate, became a magnificent city with 400 mosques and a population of half a million. Before A.D. 1000 Baghdad, on the Tigris, with miles of streetlighting, was the largest city in the world.

The process of reconstruction in Europe after the invasions was greatly helped by the monasteries which had preserved and handed down Roman technology; consequently, they became the centers of research and experimentation in many spheres of knowledge.

Craftwork, especially in metal, required heat for energy. Because Europe was still mostly covered by huge forests, wood was in plentiful supply. Although widespread deforestation which took place to provide this raw material created new farmlands, it did not allow time or space for fresh growth. Because wood now had to be found farther and farther afield at an increasing expense, coal mining developed.

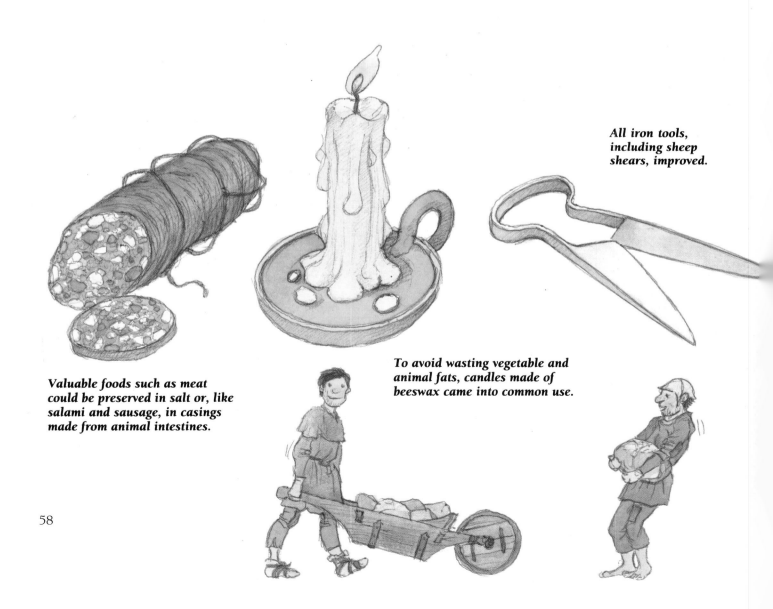

All iron tools, including sheep shears, improved.

Valuable foods such as meat could be preserved in salt or, like salami and sausage, in casings made from animal intestines.

To avoid wasting vegetable and animal fats, candles made of beeswax came into common use.

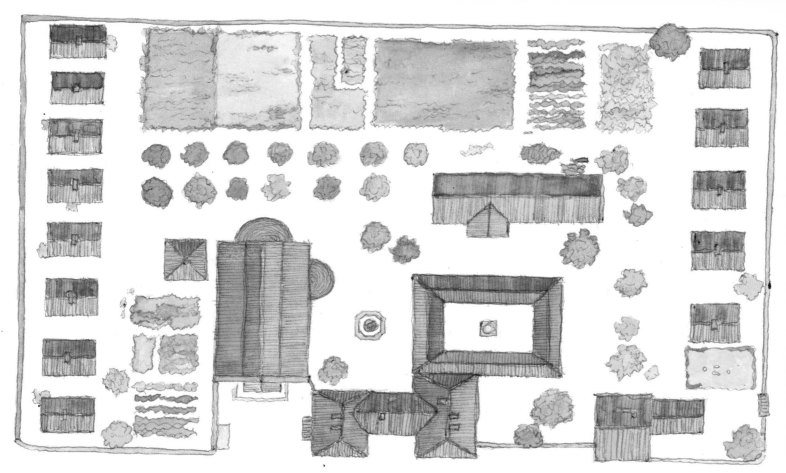

Monasteries resembled highly organized villages; they had a church, a library, a refectory, and a cloister in the center. The cells where the monks slept surrounded the cloister, while workshops of every description were at the back.

To convert wood into charcoal, branches were heaped over a fireplace and covered with earth, but with an opening left in the top, and then the fire was lit. As the slowly burning wood dried out, the carbon was retained.

Only about a quarter of the 80,000 men in the barbarian hordes that invaded the Roman Empire were fighting men. They didn't coordinate action among themselves, nor did they advance with any definite plan. When a campaign to reconquer Italy was launched from Constantinople, the capital of the Eastern Roman Empire, it initially met with success. A reconciliation of the Germanic and Roman worlds was attempted first by the Ostrogoths, and then by the Franks; this reconciliation was sealed by mass conversions to Christianity, as well as by agreements with the pope, the only authority who could give official approval to a new central power.

The great strength of the Germanic and Slavic troops lay not so much in deployment and tactics as in the speed and force of their attack, not to mention their personal prowess and courage in combat. While the Roman cavalry had served only as an effective backup force, horses now became a central element in warfare. Although the long sword was the most widely used weapon, arms and armor hadn't yet become formalized; they varied from group to group, some of them even incorporating Roman features. Contemporary records describe particularly ferocious bands of warriors who wore helmets shaped like heads of bears, wolves, dogs, and other animals; these were based on old ritual masks originally used for the festivities of the supreme god, Woden, or Odin.

Thick clothing and furs were needed
in the harsh northern climate.
Although saddles were considered a
luxury in battle, horses were
protected from the cold by
saddlecloths.

Armor made of interlocking iron
rings was copied from the
Romans. Because few could afford
such armor, a breastplate of thick
leather or fur was more commonly
used.

The Free Commununes

The Germanic empire never really succeeded in uniting all of western Europe under one king. Its greatest enemy was the papacy, which occasionally allied itself with external forces who opposed the empire. The papacy also supported internal forces represented by the more highly developed cities which, declaring their autonomy, were determined to dissolve the empire's unity. This centuries-long struggle, which finally came to a head when Emperor Frederick II occupied southern Italy, began with the battle over *investiture,* the appointment of bishops, in these cities.

The empire managed to survive only because of the tribute that was raised from the richer cities of the Rhineland and northern Italy. These areas, which had little liking for imperial authority and even less liking for the great feudal lords and lord-bishops, united on several occasions in armed conflict against the imperial army.

Because of the rivalry between the various communes,

The mercantile class, which grew ever wealthier as trade increased, often allied themselves with the bishop. Their trade guilds and corporations became powerful bodies with a strong voice in city government.

Emperors were elected, often with fierce rivalry and corruption, by the upper nobility. These nobles handed down both titles and possessions within their families, thus establishing a hereditary aristocracy.

European unity was occasionally achieved during the Crusades, when all kingdoms united against a common enemy, the Saracens. However, as free commercial enterprise increased in importance, taking up arms against the Saracens became less of a concern.

Peasants, who still made up the majority of the population, experienced a considerable improvement in their standard of living. Fortunately, as population increased, food production kept pace without serious shortages.

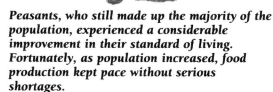

republics, and free cities, the sovereign always had plenty of room in which to maneuver. The fierce battles which raged within these political groups resulted in the emergence of two opposing forces, one aristocratic and faithful to the emperor, the other made up of rich entrepreneurs and merchants who allied themselves with the papacy.

The governments of the free communes had to strike a balance among rival factions, or at least reach a compromise. Laws regulating life in the city were proclaimed, and a council in each city elected the supreme magistrates, whose titles varied according to local traditions. Associated with these magistrates in some Italian city-states was a *capitano del popolo,* an outsider with no direct interests in the city who led the common people and safeguarded their concerns. The third most influential entity in the city, both morally and politically, was the bishop.

The emerging middle class was the most vital element in the free communes; the wealth of the city depended on its professional skills and energy. The fine new buildings of this period were constructed for this new segment of the population.

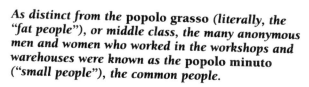

As distinct from the popolo grasso (literally, the "fat people"), or middle class, the many anonymous men and women who worked in the workshops and warehouses were known as the popolo minuto ("small people"), the common people.

Medieval society, at its zenith in the thirteenth century, expressed its vitality in a tremendous burst of building. Roman towns were rebuilt, enlarged, and circled with new walls that included outlying villages. With the great increase in both population and wealth, new towns sprang up in previously rural areas. In the center of these towns were magnificent cathedrals and town halls; they symbolized the independence and power of the guilds which vied with each other in their construction.

Even small towns, which were occupied mostly by artisans and tradesmen, were fortified with bastions, walls, and gates. In hilly areas, the highest places were chosen for building sites as being easier to defend, although the rural population took refuge in the towns when there were raids from other communes or when invasion threatened from the East or from the sea. The rural nobility, who owned castles set in woodlands and gardens in the country, and tall towers that were half house and half castle in the towns, also claimed their rights in the towns. Rival families with bands of followers often met in the streets to fight out their endless feuds.

Aside from the large market square, the public areas of medieval towns and cities were no larger than was needed for pedestrians and traffic. Following the natural terrain of the land, the streets were often tortuous and steep, a factor that would aid in the defense of the town in the event that an enemy penetrated the gates.

Ownership of town land was carefully allotted, with buildings erected accordingly. Because lots were long and narrow, the shops that lined the main streets had their storehouses and workshops in back and living quarters upstairs.

Papal and imperial factions were in continual conflict, and whenever either group came into power, it would demolish the fortified towers of the other. When rival families obtained control of a town, they ordered enemy towers to be reduced in height. This explains why so few medieval towers still stand in Italy's old commune cities; one notable exception is the Tuscan town of San Gimignano, where fourteen towers stand to this day. Eventually the building of new towers was made illegal.

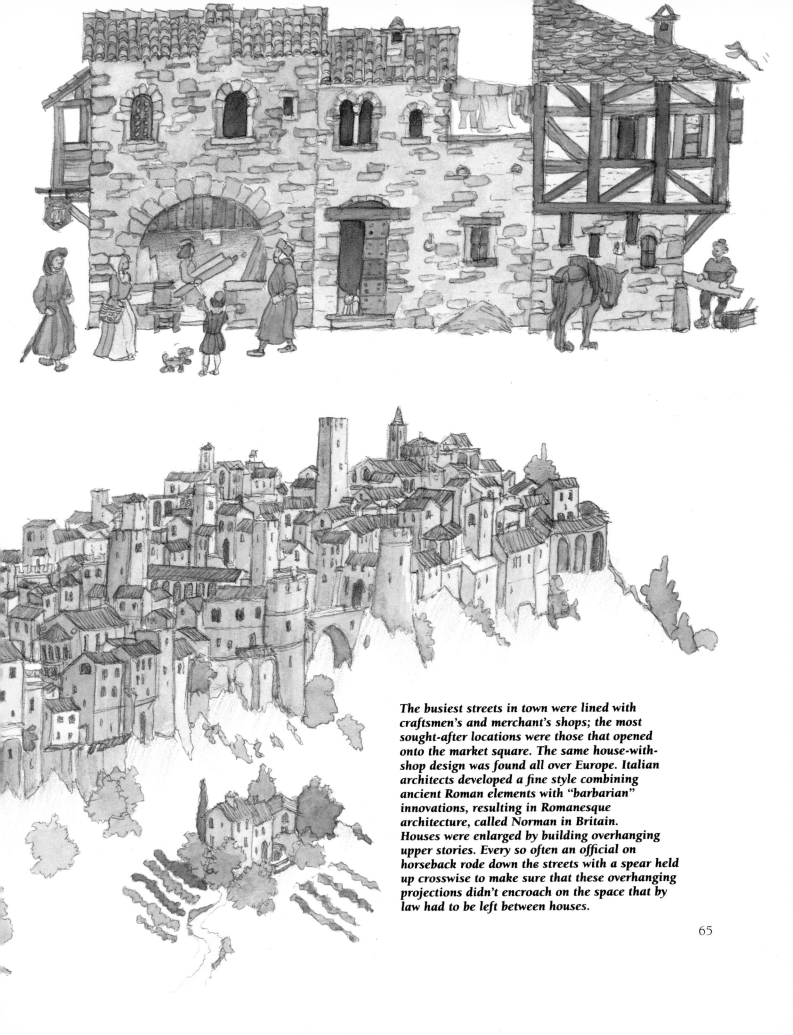

The busiest streets in town were lined with craftsmen's and merchant's shops; the most sought-after locations were those that opened onto the market square. The same house-with-shop design was found all over Europe. Italian architects developed a fine style combining ancient Roman elements with "barbarian" innovations, resulting in Romanesque architecture, called Norman in Britain. Houses were enlarged by building overhanging upper stories. Every so often an official on horseback rode down the streets with a spear held up crosswise to make sure that these overhanging projections didn't encroach on the space that by law had to be left between houses.

The remarkable economic and cultural expansion in Europe between about 950 and 1300 was due in large part to improvements in farming. Once vast areas of land had been deforested and prepared for tilling, the peasants were assigned plots on an increasingly regular basis, in exchange for fixed corvée, which enabled them to grow more than enough produce for their own needs. Thus, by having goods for barter, they were in a position to make money, which in turn allowed them to buy goods once available only to the nobility. In order to produce more, the farmers needed ever better tools, and this created business for the metalworkers. If additional farmhands were needed, instead of hiring help the farmer and his wife produced more children to carry on their work. Under a patriarchal family system, the population boomed and once again an agricultural tradition developed, with various specialties and styles of farming, such as seed selection, grafting, and crop rotation, emerging.

With the advent of the plowshare, only one plowing was necessary. Long, narrow strips of land were given to individual farmers on either side of a central road. As dwellings grew up along this road, the medieval farming village evolved.

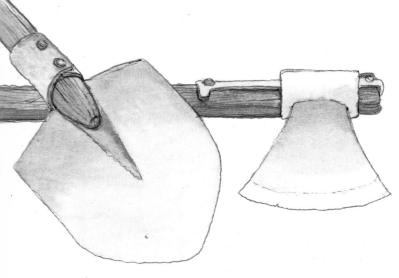

66

Developments in crafts benefited agriculture. Two inventions in particular were significant: the chest harness with a padded collar for draft horses, and the articulated plow with an iron moldboard, which made it possible to plow more deeply. Now not only the nobility patronized the saddler and the blacksmith, the ordinary farmer did as well.

In addition to bread and traditional alcoholic drinks, wine in the south and beer in the north, the diet of farming families throughout Europe was based largely on the pig, which provided both meat and fat.

In Mediterranean countries where the dry land had only a shallow layer of humus, deep plowing was not necessary. Central Europe and eastern Europe, with plenty of water and rich, clayey, vegetative soil, became the great producers of cereals.

The growth of population and agricultural productivity resulted in a steady shift in the work force, from the land into different trades. At the same time, the farmers' increased purchasing power created a new demand for craftwork, thus providing artisans with more income. During the thirteenth century, numerous self-employed artisans, who by now had become rich and influential, organized themselves into corporations, or *guilds,* to protect their interests and keep a check on what the various workshops were producing. Because the different trades now had to be recognized by their respective guilds, it was no longer possible simply to declare oneself an artisan such as a chemist or a weaver. The guilds issued laws regulating the quality of production and decided the terms on which producers could share the market. Representing a considerable force, the guilds had a strong financial and political voice in running towns and cities.

Every trade had its jealously guarded secrets. This legitimate form of self-protection not only led to conservatism but also did nothing to encourage new ideas and inventions. The idea of a *patent,* which ensured that anyone could use a new invention upon payment of a certain sum to the inventor, came much later.

Most of the workers in guild workshops were day laborers who often lived and ate in the same house as their employer. To complete their training, *apprentices* went from one workshop to another and from town to town. When they had finished their training, they had to produce their *masterpiece,* an object that met the standards of the guild controlling their particular craft. Not until they had thus proved their professional skill were they recognized as *masters.* Some apprentices inherited businesses or married the boss's daughter or widow.

Farmers never favored the water mill, even though it was more efficient and produced finer flour than that ground at home with mortar and pestle or in a small domestic mill. Maybe that was because the feudal lord who built and ran the mill imposed a flour-milling tax.

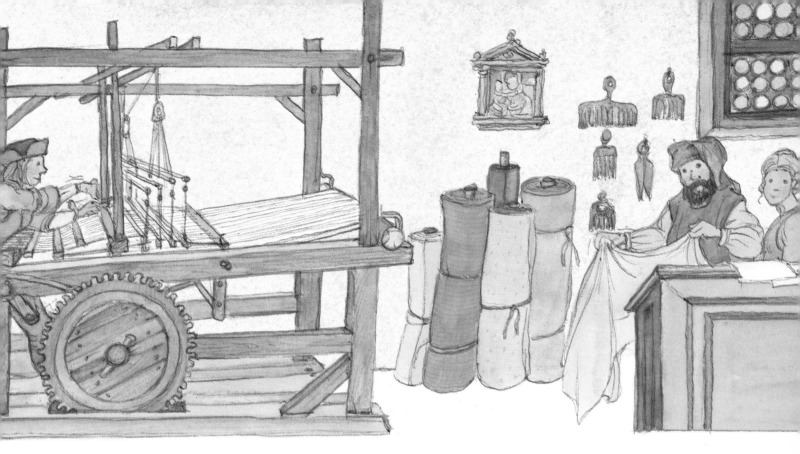

Loom weaving was a complex process. Over the pre-prepared warp of threads, the woof was woven by a shuttle loaded with more thread, while moving combs, which regulated the design of the cloth, were operated by pedals.

Distilling alcohol from wine required some chemical know-how, as well as special equipment that only pharmacists and monks possessed. Regarded as the quintessence of the wine from which it had been distilled, such alcohol was known as aqua vitae, or water of life. Later, fermented cereals were similarly distilled to produce whiskey.

The merchant class became powerful in the free cities. No longer mere shopkeepers who bought and sold goods that happened to be brought to their town, they became large-scale entrepreneurs, shipowners, and patrons of fairs and markets, and their warehouses were filled with goods of all kinds.

After the Crusades, closer links were established with the East, thus reopening a substantial market. Seaports, their livelihood based on trade, had supplied shops and money to the crusading knights. The silk road, open again, led from the port of Rostov on the Black Sea, through Samarkand, and on to the Mongol Empire and Peking. Venice, one of the greatest cities of Europe and *the* port to the East, was isolated and protected by its lagoon. Governed as an independent republic, it reaped great profits from its maritime trade. In northern Europe, trade on the Baltic was monopolized by German Hanseatic League cities. German merchants established major trading centers in London, in Bruges, Flanders, and in Novgorod, Russia.

Because of poor roads and the expense of tolls and duties, transportation by land was more of a problem. The more successful merchants managed to negotiate exemptions and monopolies in exchange for money loans to local lords, and they made use of the great trade fairs, which by tradition remained free.

Nevertheless, most transportation of valuable goods was still risky and merchants were careful to have solid capital behind them, or to have money available to them from other merchants in distant towns. Banks evolved from these needs, both to look after the money of clients who entrusted the banks with their fortunes and to lend money to those clients whom the banks trusted. The major merchants, with their own money benches (the word *bank* derives from the Italian *banco,* or "bench"), were also bankers. Florence and Siena were particularly renowned as banking cities.

Letters of credit from a well-known bank were as valuable as money. Because there were certain Church laws against usury, careful formulas had to be worked out to determine acceptable interest rates on loans.

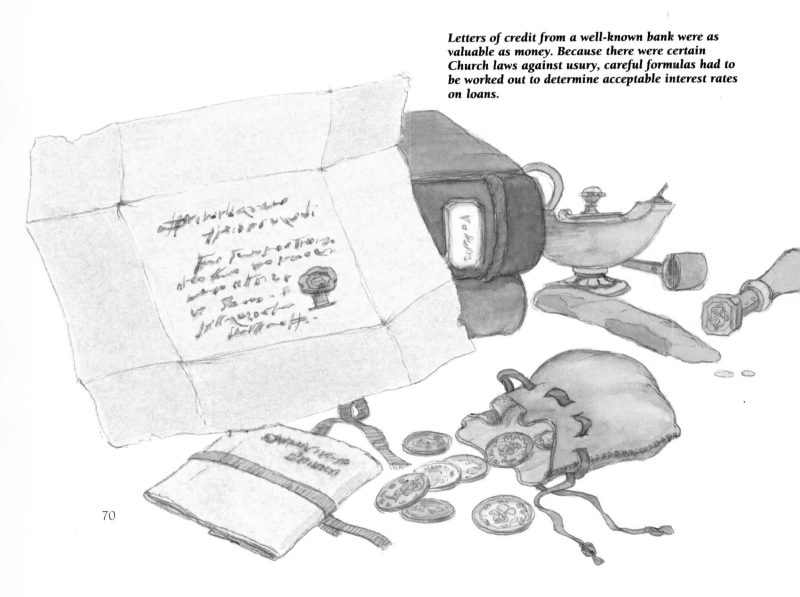

70

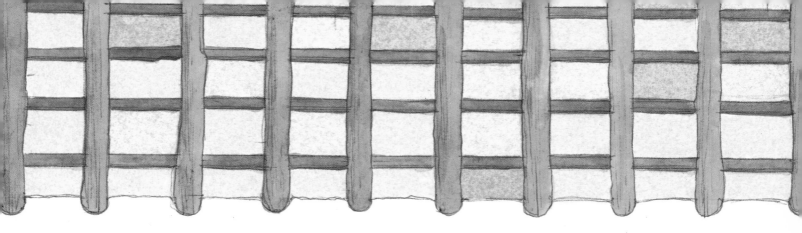

The economy of naval republics such as Pisa, Genoa, and Venice in Italy and of the German Hanseatic cities with their capital at Lübeck was based completely on trade. Although the center of commerce between Venice and Lübeck was originally at Bruges, in Flanders, it had to be moved to Antwerp when the port at Bruges became too full of silt. Venetians always had spices and silks from the East for sale, while Lübeck offered wools and Russian furs. Ships from the south sailed with cargoes of fruit, oil, wine, and woolen cloth, while ships arrived from the north laden with minerals, barreled fish, and wool for weaving.

As the textile industry flourished, tailors of the thirteenth century worked with fine wools, soft silks, heavy velvets, and cottons light as gauze, as well as luxury fabrics from the newly reopened Eastern markets. Fur trim on clothing became popular as far south as Italy.

In Italy, women wore a long, tight tunic with clinging sleeves and a loose overgarment with sleeves that widened at the wrist to reveal the different fabric and color of the tunic beneath. The neckline, which was wide and low-cut, was edged with embroidery or different-colored material. Toward the end of the thirteenth century, women began to cut their hair, but until then, they wore it loose, pinning it with small garlands or covering it with a transparent veil.

French women wore a light tunic with tight sleeves and an embroidered neckline, over which they donned a flowing embroidered coat which was belted at the waist and had sleeves that reached to the ground. Over their shoulders they wore a cape with a short train.

Women in the north imitated Italian and French fashions, the difference being that their overgarment had side slits to reveal the tunic underneath and did not have sleeves. On their heads they wore a stylized crown with a wimple hanging from it which framed the face.

Men also wore two tunics, with massive leather belts studded with metal for decoration. The tights they wore instead of breeches had no pockets, so that wallets or purses hung at the belt or were slung from the shoulder.

Fashions in the fourteenth century became even more elaborate. To "streamline" their bodies, women's clothing became tighter under the breasts and swept down into long trains. Sleeves were puffed and hemmed, and headwear—in the form of caps, turbans, bonnets, and hoods—became extravagant; in fact, the town council of Lyons even condemned the frivolity of certain headwear.

Typical hairstyles of the Middle Ages

The number and type of materials, colors, and accessories worn by an individual varied according to his or her social class. Bright colors such as scarlet, and certain shades of blue and green, were forbidden to the common people, for example. Workmen used certain kinds of cloth, friars used other kinds, and servants used cloth with striped bands. Pilgrims (in Italian pellegrini) wore a short cape, called a pellegrina, over their shoulders.

73

With Europe divided, and Saracens to be found on all its southern shores, pirates roamed the once safe and peaceful Mediterranean. As merchant ships had to learn to defend themselves, the difference between warships and trading vessels disappeared and small fortified "castles" (the forecastle and quarterdeck) were built at bow and stern. It was just such ships with "castles" that King Louis IX of France hired when he led a Crusade.

Spanish merchant ships introduced the lateen sail, which had probably been used on Byzantine ships originally. It was a modified version of the square sail, with the yardarm slanted and the bottom edge of the sail shortened in order to catch contrary winds, making it possible to sail against the wind. The single flat rudder mounted at the stern replaced twin steering oars so that now ships could be steered easily from a seat on the quarterdeck. To counterbalance a second mast that was added toward the bow, a third mast was added on the quarterdeck. With all these improvements, ships were able to navigate the open seas more safely, and in fact, no sooner had the "Islamic threat" been met and dealt with once and for all than Columbus set sail for America.

A caravel

A Mediterranean galley

Horseback was still the fastest form of land travel. Saddles, stirrups, reins, bits, spurs, and harnesses were all improved to make riding safer and more comfortable. Posting stations were set up along major roads; here riders could change horses, have them reshod, or simply stop for refreshment.

The economic boom under the feudal system and in the free cities stimulated research into ways to increase production of goods and improve the quality of what was produced. Deforestation and land reclamation over vast areas such as the Black Forest and the Danube Valley created a need for large numbers of axes, saws, and moldboards. During this period tools became increasingly efficient, and advances were made in forging and tempering steel. Water energy was harnessed to power hammers by attaching cams to the shaft of the wheel, which raised the hammer and let it drop back on the anvil. This method, which made rolling iron easier and more efficient, was also used to produce pestles for papermaking and presses for fulling cloth.

Animal power, especially horse power, became more effective with the advent of the chest harness and stirrups. While the old leather collars posed the danger of suffocating the horse, a stuffed collar afforded maximum use of the horse's strong pectoral muscles.

When Rome collapsed, many ancient skills were lost, especially in the manufacture of textiles, glassware, and ceramics. However, because these old skills survived in the Byzantine and Islamic worlds, they were reintroduced to Europe by the Arabs, and they began to develop once again there.

The Benedictine monasteries played a fundamental role as research centers for all forms of industry as well as agriculture. No large abbey functioned without a cellar, a brewery, a lime kiln, a mill, and countless workshops. The monks, from the herbalist to the artisan to the launderer to the tanner, practiced their trades here. Because the monastic movement expanded rapidly and close contact was maintained among monasteries, new inventions introduced in monasteries spread quickly all over Europe.

The new padded horse collar

An iron plowshare, which cut deeply into the earth

Roads were barely passable for animal-drawn vehicles, so saddles and stirrups, which were almost essential for comfort, came into common use.

A water hammer

77

As Europe began to find some stability after centuries of battling between Germanic kings, a fresh wave of invasions of Vikings, Magyars, and Saracens broke from the north and east. Once again Europe was plunged into long and exhausting wars, and whole armies were occupied for years in the East during the Crusades. The political agreements that followed led to a division of the continent into separate, mutually antagonistic kingdoms such as France and England, which were at each other's throats for a hundred years. Even the free cities, communes, and more or less autonomous principalities within the kingdoms fought each other often over land, money, or political power. Certainly men who wanted to be soldiers in the early centuries of the second millennium A.D. found no lack of opportunity.

Every feudal lord kept his own small army of guards which was increased in time of war by all the vassals to whom the lord had granted privileges and concessions. If necessary, even farmers were mobilized to protect the growing prosperity they enjoyed in their fief.

From childhood, male children of the nobility were trained in arms. The eldest son would succeed his father as the next lord and chief of the army. The other sons had to use their fighting ability to make their own way in the world; they would serve one of the greater lords faithfully, and he would in turn reward them with fiefs of their own.

A knight was armed with a lance over twelve feet long, a studded iron mace, an ax, and a broadsword; the sword was often given a name, just like the knight's trusty steed.

A crossbow

In the age of chivalry, knights championed Christianity, justice, and honor; the chivalric ideal was the subject of epic poetry and heroic tales for centuries. Knights swore loyalty unto death to their code of honor rather than to their lord.

A bolt

The knight wore chain mail and plate armor, and the plumes on his helmet and decoration on his shield made him a gallant sight indeed!

Monarchs Great and Small

England and France, at war with each other in the fourteenth and fifteenth centuries, eventually established their respective kingdoms, while the German empire splintered into small independent duchies and principalities. Taking advantage of this constant state of chaos, the leading families in the free communes could gain control.

After the death of the last great emperor, Charles V, in 1558, Europe was split into a number of different states, some large and some small, each governed by its own monarch. The only republic to survive was Venice, with a second republic, Holland, soon to rise in the Low Countries. Although the pope was also secular sovereign over his own recognized Church state, the Reformation brought a challenge to his spiritual authority. Europe was soon deeply divided between Catholic and Protestant

With constant mobilization, armies made up of mercenaries commanded by professional officers became stable military units.

In return for their homage and promised loyalty, aristocrats acquired many privileges, such as recognition at court. But the most important government positions went to the king's powerful ministers, those able diplomats who best understood how to influence and guide their sovereigns' political decisions.

Lawyers and bureaucrats were in a class above the common people.

states, with religious wars the inevitable and tragic result. Territorial aggression, dynastic claims, religious wars, and social unrest all led to continuing armed conflict.

Production in the Middle Ages had generally been a communal effort as well as a common creative achievement. Now individuals who were to become universally renowned as artists and scholars began to emerge from the guilds. Beginning in Italy, the great cultural renewal known as the Renaissance spread throughout all of Europe. Michelangelo, Leonardo, and Raphael emerged as artists whose names will always evoke this remarkable period of history when the human spirit reached its highest expression. Other equally famous Renaissance figures are Columbus and Galileo, whose names have come to symbolize man's freedom and inner faith in the search beyond the known to the unknown, in the exploration and observation of the world and the cosmos.

During the same period, the great poets and playwrights Ariosto, Shakespeare, Tasso, and Molière were writing works that have helped people through the ages to examine and understand the deep mystery that is the human soul. Even the "art" of politics found theoretical formulation in Machiavelli's *The Prince,* while Castiglione's *The Book of the Courtier* set a universal example of elegance and perfect manners. The great achievements in the material world, such as the advances in seafaring, mining, agriculture, weaving, and various crafts, should not be overlooked.

Artists and scientists of Renaissance courts

This great new rebirth of civilization in Europe followed a period of constant crisis and decadence, a period which had been marked by famine and plague for most of the fourteenth century.

The sense of rebirth (for this is what *renaissance* means) which spread from Italy to France and from there throughout Europe found architectural expression in the rediscovery of the Greco-Roman past and a reinterpretation of classical styles. Ideal cities were conceived, and although these were based on abstract geometrical perfection, certain practical improvements such as using space wisely were also taken into account. The mazelike streets of medieval cities, which were criticized for being dingy and unhealthy, were now replaced by open spaces, squares and great wide streets lined with fine town houses.

Dynasties, both large and small, enjoyed absolute power, which meant that it was possible to build palaces the likes of which had not been seen since Roman times.

The aristocracy too constructed grand houses decorated with superb works of art. Florence, with its splendid buildings and country villas, which were themselves small palaces, demonstrated among the finest examples of this renewal. In the Veneto, the northern Italian region governed by Venice, an architectural style emerged that all of Europe studied and imitated.

Farther north, Gothic architecture remained fashionable for centuries. Techniques of half-timbering were developed to such an extent that woodworking became as decorative as embroidery, while in the Low Countries, where wood was less plentiful, handsome buildings were made of brick.

The greatest changes in urban planning came somewhat later, in the seventeenth century, when outstanding development programs were undertaken in Rome under Pope Urban VIII, in Amsterdam with its three concentric canals, and in London after the Great Fire of 1666.

The Gothic tradition in building lasted for centuries in northern Europe. The Tudor style in England coexisted with the new architecture of Inigo Jones, who was greatly inspired by the Italian Renaissance.

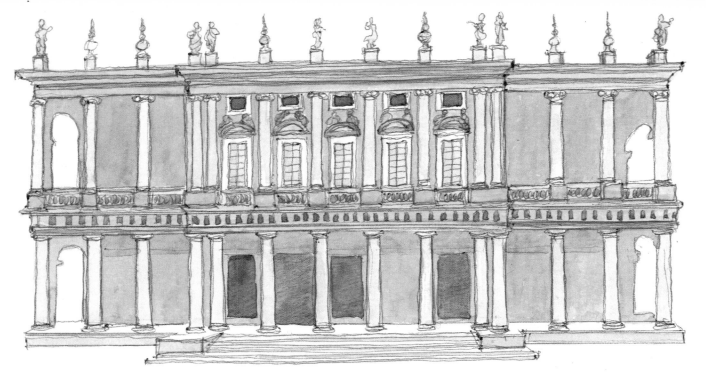

After the Great Fire, London was completely rebuilt in brick and stone in a style adapted from the Italian classical revival, more particularly from the work of the great architect Andrea Palladio in the Veneto. This same style was later "exported" to the American colonies.

The half-timbered houses lining the main thoroughfare of German towns often had their own names; these were taken from the name of the family who lived in the building; from the sign over the entrance; from the use the public made of the building; or even from the pennant on the roof.

After the crisis years of the fourteenth century, the burden of recovery, as usual, fell on the farmers, although it was not until the sixteenth century, and in some places even later, that agriculture came into its own again. When German peasants, who lived under intolerable conditions, rebelled en masse, they were harshly and quickly suppressed by both secular and Church authorities.

Conditions were much better in the Low Countries. As the population grew, more land was made available through painstaking reclamation from the sea by an elaborate process of drainage and dike building. Those who worked on these projects acquired partial ownership of the reclaimed land, where intensive small-scale farming techniques proved to be very effective. The Dutch peasants, now as rich and respected as other working classes, were the first farmers in Europe to have some representation on property councils.

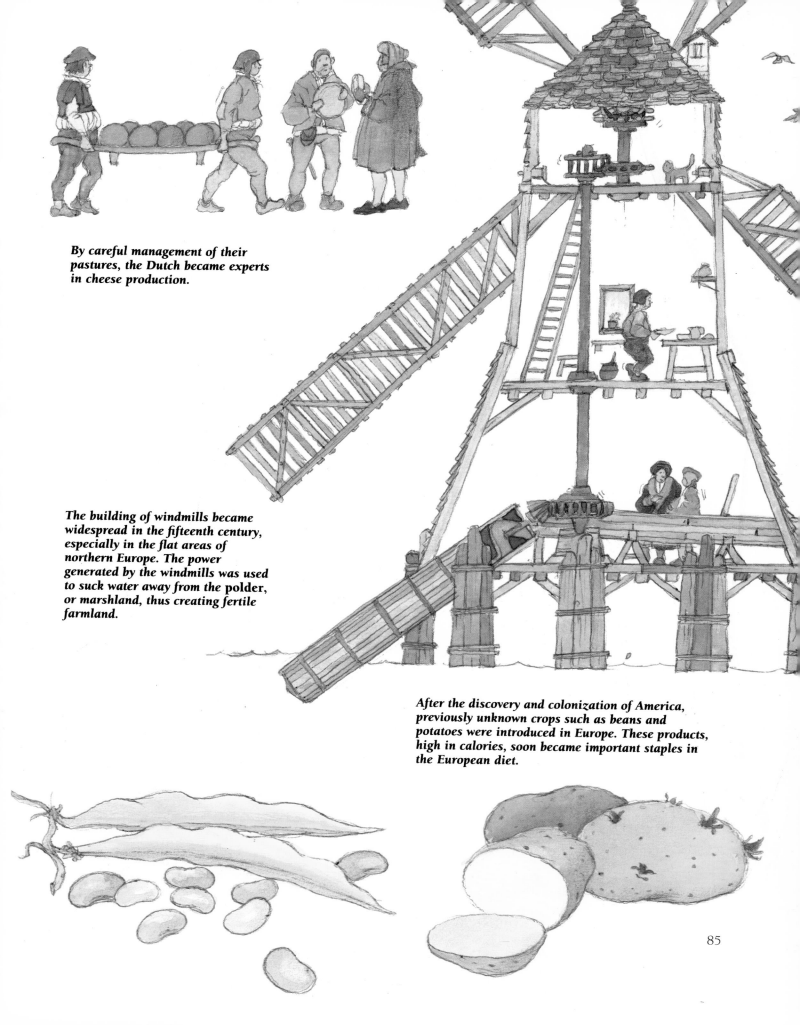

By careful management of their pastures, the Dutch became experts in cheese production.

The building of windmills became widespread in the fifteenth century, especially in the flat areas of northern Europe. The power generated by the windmills was used to suck water away from the polder, or marshland, thus creating fertile farmland.

After the discovery and colonization of America, previously unknown crops such as beans and potatoes were introduced in Europe. These products, high in calories, soon became important staples in the European diet.

Not only did the invention of the printing press in the mid-fifteenth century revolutionize the dispersal of information, but it was also part of a whole new manufacturing process which grew quickly right from the start. By the beginning of the sixteenth century, only fifty years after the invention of the printing press, some eight million books had been printed, more than had been copied by hand since the earliest days of writing.

Printing was highly specialized work which involved casting movable characters, composing pages, and preparing paper before the actual process of printing with a hand press even began. Books then had to be bound and the fine leather bindings decorated. Consequently, affiliated trades also developed to produce, for example, paper and special inks that wouldn't blur.

The production of paper, which was invented by the Chinese and brought to Europe by the Arabs, became an important business only after the invention of the printing press. Paper was made by soaking and grinding vegetable fibers such as flax or cotton in water and then pulping them, recovering the waste for later use. The remaining paste, which was filtered from the water, was spread on frames that were the same size as the desired sheet size and was then compressed. After a thorough drying, the sheets were ready for the printer.

Glass production expanded greatly during this period, especially in cities such as Venice, whose island of Murano soon became world-famous for its glass. The glassblower's tools were simple: an iron pipe to blow through and an iron support which was applied red-hot to the glass object to keep it malleable so it could be worked with tongs and shears. Fine glassware depended entirely on the skill of the glassblower.

With the spread of copper engravings, pictures by famous artists now became more widely known through engraved reproductions. Printing from an engraved copper plate was based on the same technique as printing the written word; the plate was inked with a roller and then pressed against the paper in a hand press.

Pulped fibers steeped in water and ground with pestles produced the paste for papermaking. Although the pestles were operated by a handle, in larger businesses a water wheel was used. At the far right in the illustration is the frame on which the paste was spread to make a sheet of paper.

At the center of the glassmaker's workshop were both the casting furnace for melting the raw materials, sodium carbonate and sand, and the reheating furnace used for joining the different parts of the finished product. A variety of earthenware or copper molds completed the glassmaker's equipment.

In the years following Charlemagne's reform of the monetary system, the silver *denarius* was reduced in value as it became lighter in weight; this was due, in part, to the difficulty of finding enough silver to meet the growing demand. Because different communes, principalities, and republics had their own mints, differently weighted currency appeared, none of which bore any relationship to the original *libbra,* the original standard pound weight for gold or silver. The need for a more stable coinage, which was already felt by the mid-thirteenth century, resulted in the Florentine gold florin and the Venetian gold ducat, both of which were soon in use all over Europe. The importance of gold became apparent by the sixteenth century, when the florin, which was originally worth one *lira,* escalated to a worth of seven *lire.* To reestablish some sort of stability, the gold *scudo* was minted.

Only with the financial backing of the now enormously wealthy banks were the great expeditions to India and the West Indies possible. These voyages were undertaken to find treasure and cheap gold, as the Spanish did in Mexico and Peru and the Portuguese did in the African Gold Coast.

Exploration led to colonization, which in turn created an extensive and very profitable trading network that spanned the continents. Spanish traders sailed their galleons from Acapulco in Mexico to Manila in the Philippines, where they exchanged their cargoes of silver for silk. Sugar cane, once grown on the Mediterranean coasts, was introduced into Brazil by the Portuguese. Unfortunately, because the new plantations were worked by slaves forcibly imported from Africa, the trading of human beings again became a flourishing business.

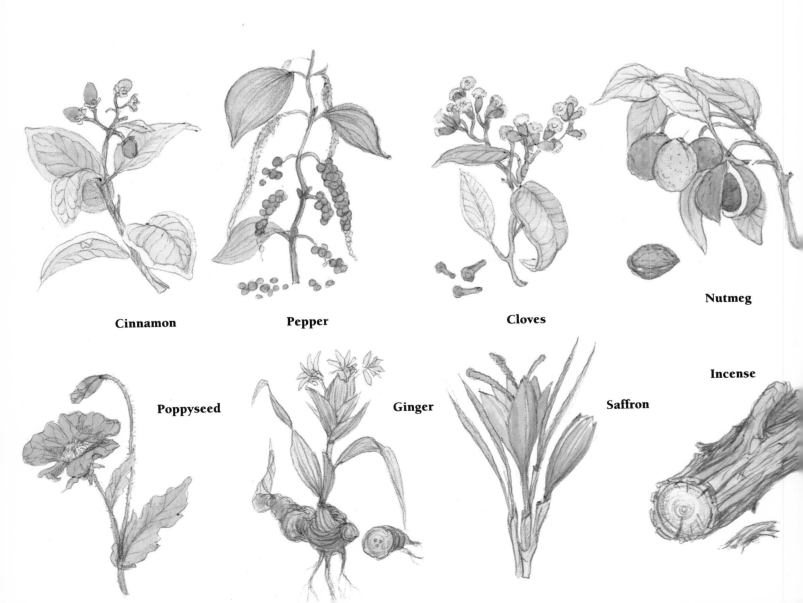

Cinnamon

Pepper

Cloves

Nutmeg

Poppyseed

Ginger

Saffron

Incense

Lorenzo de' Medici, called the Magnificent

Jakob Fugger II

The economic strength of the banks had direct political impact. In Florence the Medici family established first a signoria, or lordship, then a grand duchy; they also provided France with two queens and Rome with three popes. In Augsburg,

Germany, the Fugger family even helped the Emperor Charles V financially when he was having trouble paying his troops. The basis of the financial success of these two families lay in their knowledge of and representation in all the major markets.

Here a money changer works at his scales. Worn-out coins were bought according to their weight and then melted down.

A new fashion was introduced, the Spanish *vertugado*, which was originally just an underskirt widened at the bottom by means of whalebone ribs. In France, however, it soon evolved into a great drum held up by a metal hoop around the hips, and waists were made tiny with excruciating corsets—Caterina de' Medici recommended an eighteen-inch waist. The bodice, which was tight and often adorned with precious stones, pearls, and gold and ivory buttons, had a low, square-cut neckline that stretched from shoulder to shoulder; magnificent interchangeable puffed sleeves were slashed to show a linen or silk blouse underneath. In contrast, headgear became less elaborate, with the hair styled short or gathered up in a fine veil or net.

Shirts became standard for men; slightly curled collars gradually became more elaborate, finally evolving into the extravagantly starched *ruff.* Horsehair or hay padding was used on the shoulders and in the breast of the *doublet,* a close-fitting coat worn over breeches. Breeches were now gathered over stockings either above or below the knee, and like sleeves, they were cut with slits called "slashings," through which brilliantly colored silk linings spilled out. For headgear men wore flat velvet or brocade caps with a small brim and plumes.

Although women also wore ruffs, they favored stiff lace collars that fanned up to hide their necklines.

German women rejected the *vertugado,* ruff, and double sleeves and instead wore veils with coifs, close-fitting caps like those of nuns, and long pleated dresses of rich material with the neckline of the bodice decorated with fabric. Women in the Netherlands wore similar fashions; their coifs, however, which were stretched on a small frame with the veil attached by needlework and jewelry, were broader.

**Clothes worn
to play tennis**

Clothes were stitched while on the wearer. Padding and metal hoops, which widened skirts, made waists look smaller. Starched muslin ruffs grew so large, it is said, that spoon handles had to be made longer so that people could reach their mouths.

Shoes, either of soft leather or fine material, were generally comfortable, although Venetian records mention pattens, or clogs, and shoes that were designed with heels almost six inches high, perhaps with the high-tide floods of Venice in mind!

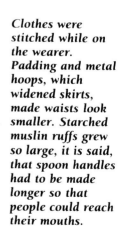

European expansion overseas was a driving force in the sixteenth and seventeenth centuries. In only a few decades, Spain gained control of all of Central America and the Philippines, while by the mid-sixteenth century, Portugal had some fifty mercantile and military bases up and down the African and Asian coasts. As France and England struggled over their possessions in North America, the seventeenth century saw the Dutch East India Company become the most powerful European presence in the Orient.

For at least two centuries, the European countries that bordered the Atlantic battled over their overseas colonies, until finally, with the defeat of Holland and Spain, England won control of the high seas. With this kind of turmoil going on, it isn't hard to imagine why both merchant and fighting fleets had to be expanded.

Crossing the Atlantic or rounding the Cape of Good Hope was difficult, to say the least; the journey was seemingly endless and the food was so poor that the shortage of vitamins often caused potentially fatal diseases such as scurvy. In addition to the perils of the sea itself, there was always the threat of attack by pirates or enemy ships, a danger that forced vessels to arm themselves with cannon, harquebuses, and mortars.

Traveling by land wasn't much more comfortable. The earliest coaches were mounted on the axles of iron-ringed wheels without any suspension, so that even a short journey on the rough roads of the day was a bone-shaking venture. Not until the middle of the sixteenth century was the coach suspended on leather straps, and actual springs did not appear until much later. Despite improvements, frequent stops were necessary for the comfort of the passengers for whom such travel was still a novelty.

In mid-sixteenth-century Paris, there were only three coaches, one for the queen, one for the king's mistress, and one for a nobleman who was granted permission by the king to travel by carriage because he was too fat to ride a horse.

In this cross-section of a small galleon, the recently invented pump that removed bilge water can be seen. The large hold is filled with barrels of wet sand that served as ballast to stabilize the ship. On the top deck an officer takes a sighting with a sextant; below, in his cabin, the captain writes in his logbook; and below the captain's cabin, the helmsman steers while a sailor stands ready to throw the lead line.

The discovery of new continents and the new understanding of the cosmos based on the theories of Copernicus, the founder of modern astronomy, stimulated the invention of new objects to help research and measure physical, geographical, and astronomical phenomena, and thus, modern science, based on practical experimentation and statistical comparison, was born.

The mechanical clock, a recent invention that underwent steady improvement, incorporated the pendulum principle as explored by Galileo. Lenses, which had been used for glasses since the thirteenth century, were also improved, and with the telescope, which was invented in Holland, Galileo not only discovered the moons of Jupiter, but, in his studies of sunspots, also demonstrated the Copernican heliocentric system of the universe.

Leonardo da Vinci's civil and military engineering de-

signs, including theoretical machines for human flight, anticipated many inventions that required more advanced technology than was available at that time.

There were many less spectacular, although not necessarily less significant, inventions—analytic geometry, infinitesimal calculus, and mathematical logic, which was essential for physics. Theory and application went hand in hand; the need to verify new theories stimulated practical inventions and, in turn, more new theories.

Fortunately or unfortunately, the military requirements of war have always been a stimulus for invention and an incentive for developing new technology. Improvements in iron technology made it possible to build cannon strong enough to withstand explosions, allowing gunpowder, known since the Middle Ages, to be used in mortars. These new inventions in turn changed the scale of military conflict.

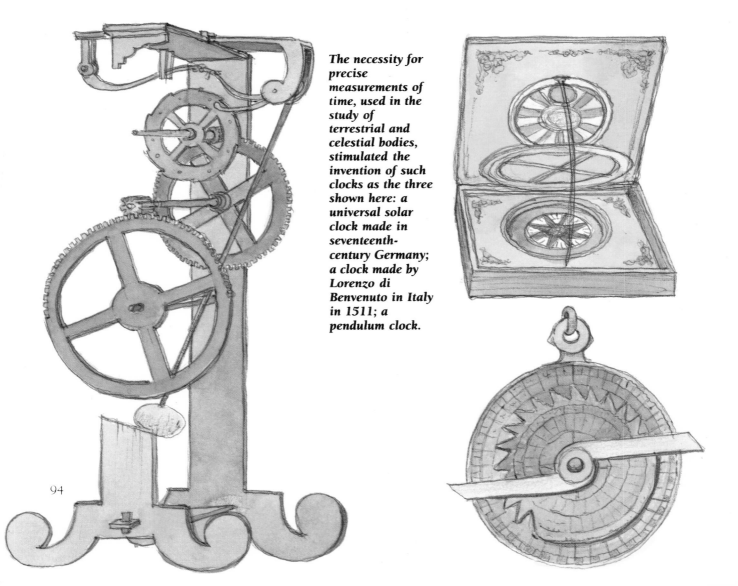

The necessity for precise measurements of time, used in the study of terrestrial and celestial bodies, stimulated the invention of such clocks as the three shown here: a universal solar clock made in seventeenth-century Germany; a clock made by Lorenzo di Benvenuto in Italy in 1511; a pendulum clock.

Galileo tried to arouse interest in the telescope, by showing how useful it could be in war. But many learned people of the time were so bound by tradition that they refused even to look into the instrument. It was the Englishman Isaac Newton who first made use of the telescope to explore the heavens.

Although firearms had been used experimentally for over a century, they developed slowly, mainly for two reasons: first, the difficulty of casting iron tubes capable of withstanding explosions, and second, the problem of producing sufficiently powerful explosives.

In the fourteenth century, the basic instrument for measuring angles was the geometric compass, which facilitated quick calculations; results were recorded on scales engraved on the two arms.

95

Each European monarch's army, whether large or small, evolved into a permanent corps which staged military parades, a new tradition that involved flags, drums, uniforms, and brilliant colors. Articulated plate armor or armor of tempered iron was common, as was the sallet helmet, which had a movable visor that protected the neck as well as the head.

In the sixteenth century, the two traditional army divisions of cavalry and infantry were joined by an equally important third, the artillery. Because the quality of a gun depended on its barrel and because its reliability depended on its firing mechanism, the first firearms were quite primitive. They were front-loading weapons to which a flame had to be applied externally; a spark from a flint would light a fuse, which in turn triggered the explosion.

The charge was rammed into the barrel with a plug and although a second plug was often used to keep the little round lead bullet in position, the bullet often rolled around inside the barrel and sometimes even rolled out before the gun was fired, making accurate aim almost impossible. With pro-longed loading time, lost bullets, and misfirings, the gun wasn't a very formidable weapon.

Cannon fire was far more effective. Large stone cannonballs, weighing up to a quintal, or roughly 220 pounds, tore huge holes in wooden ships and were equally damaging to the old medieval walls of towns and castles.

Italian plate armor

A Spanish captain

Spectacular uniforms of mercenary commanders

A German mercenary (pikeman)

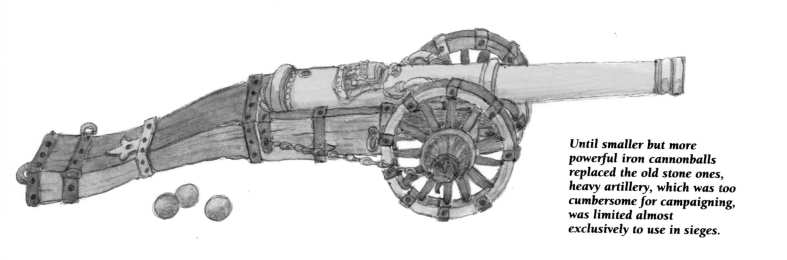

Until smaller but more powerful iron cannonballs replaced the old stone ones, heavy artillery, which was too cumbersome for campaigning, was limited almost exclusively to use in sieges.

Mercenary commanders like those on page 96 were war professionals who assembled companies of soldiers and offered them to the highest bidder. In such mercenary armies the esprit de corps was always strong.

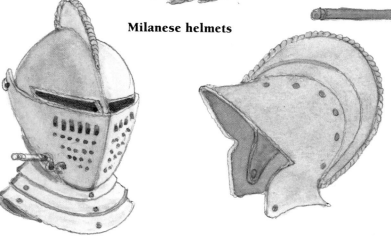

Milanese helmets

A Spanish harquebusier

Different countries gave the various types of light artillery different names. The best Italian artillery came from Venice, with its famous falcons, falconets, muskets, harquebuses, and cannon.

97

Revolution!

 In the eighteenth century the French monarchy preserved an absolutist system which allowed for a privileged class of nonproducers such as the nobility and high-level clergy, but which ignored the insistent demands of the *bourgeoisie,* the middle class, which was the most dynamic economic force in society. The notions of liberty and justice put forth by the intellectuals of the *Enlightenment* and espoused by libertarian and democratic groups led directly to the overthrow of the old regime. Toward the end of the century, a violent revolution destroyed French monarchical absolutism once and for all, sending winds of change throughout the rest of Europe.

A new military force, no longer made up of professional soldiers but drawn from the people, emerged after the French Revolution. Under Napoleon Bonaparte, this army won rapid and spectacular victories all across Europe, right into the heart of Russia.

Yet the leaders who emerged from the revolution, including Napoleon himself, with his imperial aspirations, eventually became too ambitious and had to be checked. Even though old authorities came back into power in France, the basic reforms survived, and the landowning

Gilded ladies, gallant fops, and glittering courtiers either paid for their idle and luxurious life-style under the French guillotine or fled France over roads bristling with soldiers of the national guard.

The mercantile and entrepreneurial middle classes maintained their own interests by means of trade protectionism, holding rights on colonial resources, and obtaining tax write-offs granted for industrial investments.

The common people, who were kept ignorant and illiterate, with no sense of their own rights, put up with wretched conditions in a spirit of resignation.

The landowning aristocracy fenced-in the countryside and studied new methods of production.

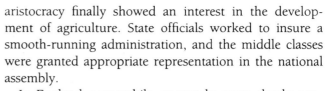

aristocracy finally showed an interest in the development of agriculture. State officials worked to insure a smooth-running administration, and the middle classes were granted appropriate representation in the national assembly.

In England, meanwhile, monarchs were clearly considered answerable to the law. King Charles I went to the block in the mid-sixteenth century for forgetting this. After the revolution led by Oliver Cromwell, Parliament, through a bill of rights, established that the king and queen "are and are considered" first among equals. In the House of Lords and the House of Commons, the two chambers of the British Parliament, all social and economic forces were represented—except the common people. Although the battle for universal suffrage still lay in the future, certain thinkers of the time began to question the right of any government to claim obedience from its citizens without granting them a say in their country's constitution. Meanwhile, the spirit of independence and free enterprise, which lay at the heart of English democracy, was flourishing far from home in the American colonies, and with the ensuing War of Independence, the United States of America came into being.

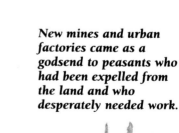

New mines and urban factories came as a godsend to peasants who had been expelled from the land and who desperately needed work.

Just as the various social classes became ever more sharply defined, so the various parts of an aristocrat's eighteenth-century town house became more clearly defined according to their function; now there were suites of "apartments." The kitchen and pantry were on the lower ground floor; reception rooms, where guests were received and formal meals eaten, on the ground floor; family living quarters on the next floor; above these, bedrooms; and finally, in the attic, servants' quarters. Although wood-burning fireplaces were built into every room, the newly invented ceramic or metal stove, fueled by either wood or coal, was used occasionally. With lighting still provided by candles, elaborately carved wooden candleholders and crystal and ceramic chandeliers came into fashion.

There were no lavatories or bathrooms, and so refuse was disposed of outdoors on dungheaps or in cesspits. As running water was not available, water had to be carried into houses and left in jugs in the bedrooms, or wherever it was needed.

With the widespread fencing-in of land, poor country folk lost some of the rights that had helped them survive, such as permission to graze, hunt, fish, and collect wood. Consequently, many of the poor drifted into the towns and cities where industry was attracting labor. These working-class people lived in modest houses packed close together, with two rooms downstairs, and a stairway leading to two bedrooms upstairs. The kitchen, which opened onto the street, became the main living room, mostly because it was the only warm room in the house.

The design of the urban English house was adopted in American cities, while the pioneers settling in the American wilderness lived in primitive log cabins built with a fireplace in the center. Guns were a necessity, as a defense against both wild animals and human marauders, although the visitor occasionally turned out to be a fur trader.

Mines, foundries, and factories
were surrounded by working-class
houses built by the factory owners.
The houses, however, were decent,
unlike the tenements and slums
that uncontrolled urbanization
would bring later.

A nobleman's house

Until the introduction of machinery, agriculture remained unchanged for centuries. Although new farming techniques evolved through scientific study and experimentation in the eighteenth century, old tools such as plows, harrows, rollers, scythes, forks, and rakes continued to be made—and improved.

In England, where there was a degree of political stability and where a population explosion produced many mouths to feed, agriculture changed radically. To achieve maximum yield from the land, fertilizers were carefully investigated and crop rotation was studied scientifically so that better harvests could be produced without impoverishing the soil. The landowning gentry and aristocracy lived close to the source of their wealth, their land, taking a direct interest in farming and trying out new ideas, with the poorer farmers following suit, to the benefit of the whole country. The fact that the English people, especially farmers, enjoyed a healthy diet more than likely contributed to their population growth as well as their longer life span.

Corn

A water mill

New crops, such as tobacco, continued to be introduced into Europe from the colonies. Corn, already brought into Europe from Russia, was grown so widely that it became a staple crop in some areas.

Coffee and tea from the East and cocoa from the Americas enriched not only the quality of life in Europe, but also the traders who dealt in them!

Tobacco

Coffee

All sorts of water-powered and hand-powered machines were redesigned to be driven by steam, a step which revolutionized production. With looms, pumps, industrial hammers, and even boats now working "under their own steam," new work patterns were needed to derive the greatest benefit from this new source of energy.

Mechanization turned the artisan into a factory hand, an unskilled worker who had no immediate contact with the finished product but who performed a repetitive task dictated by the machinery. As the quality of work dropped, the quality of the product dropped too. Nevertheless, with the increase in quantity the cost came down, broadening the market.

The primary source of energy during the steam age was coal, which meant that more and more people were needed to work in the mines. Coal mining by faint lantern light down in the bowels of the earth was certainly the toughest job of its day. With the constant danger of collapsing shafts and flooding, as well as the threat of asphyxiation and gas explosions, miners shed "blood, sweat, and tears" for their livelihood. Although animal power was still used for raising the mined coal up the shafts, children worked in the pits too, pushing small trucks along the passageways. Engine-powered machines weren't used in the mines until precise calculations indicated that the continual use of machines would be more profitable than employing manpower alone.

Great quantities of coal were used also in the production of iron, a metal that was increasingly in demand for both weapons and other functional objects. Guns and steam engines both developed slowly; their manufacture required an iron cylinder that could withstand severe and prolonged stress. It was only with the scientific advances in steel production that sufficiently strong materials were made that could withstand extreme stress.

Because the primary concern in the Industrial Revolution was productivity (the ratio of the quantity of production to the amount of time it takes to produce), it became vital to keep a strict check on time during the working day. Sunrise, midday, and sunset were signaled no longer by bells, but by mechanical clocks with springs and cogs. A new breed of craftsman emerged, the clockmaker, whose trade demanded not only a passionate love of mechanisms, but a dedication to absolute precision as well.

Horses were still used widely for all types of work, and so the power of a machine was measured in terms of horsepower, or what a horse could accomplish.

An inevitable result of all these imports flooding the European markets was that merchants, through their sheer financial strength, became the most powerful class in society. The soundest and best-known of their companies were quoted on the stock exchange, that is, titles of credit were sold to investors to raise money, with dividends paid on the returns. The titles that were bought and sold on the stock market represented small "shares" in the ownership of the business, with their value increasing or decreasing according to the success or failure of the company.

About the same time, paper money arrived on the scene. Money issued by the state no longer had to be coinage of a certain weight of gold or silver. It might simply be a piece of paper to which the state accredited a certain value, which in turn related to the reserves of gold in the national treasury.

With the discovery and conquest of lands overseas, the Mediterranean lost its importance in international trade, and as ships began to load directly from the markets of the East and West Indies, the hazardous and costly old caravan routes were gradually abandoned too. Countries bordering the Atlantic now competed for supremacy in international trade and fought sea battles for control of ports and markets, eclipsing old trade ports like Venice.

Before the industrialization of Europe, handmade goods from India and China were comparable in quality to, but a good deal cheaper than, those produced in Europe, and slave labor on large plantations in America made for intensely competitive prices.

The stock exchange was the place for those who enjoyed the risky game of speculating on the rise and fall of companies.

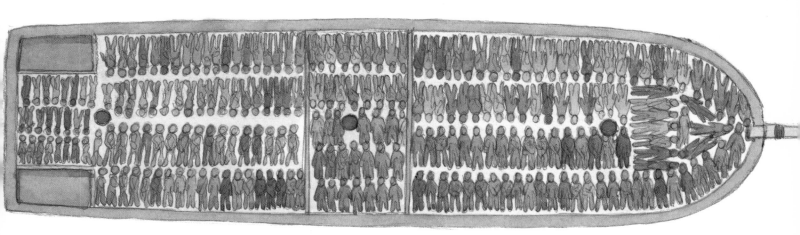

During the eighteenth century, some two million slaves were transported to British colonies alone, while the ever-expanding cotton, coffee, and cocoa plantations in the Americas required more and more slaves. Here the design of a slave ship shows how many slaves were crammed into the hold for a journey of several months; twenty percent of them would die before the ship even reached its destination.

Coffee

Cocoa

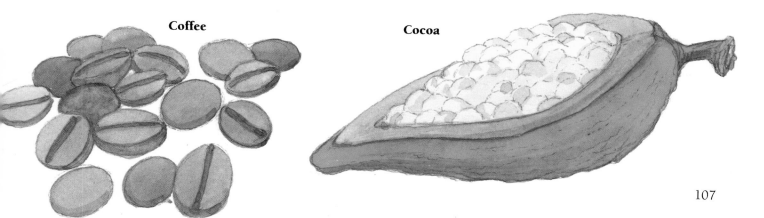

107

Eighteenth-century materials, clothes, and fashions were among the most elaborate in the history of fashion. Silk, now produced in large quantities in Europe, was the perfect material for the period. The ideal woman of that time was slender, graceful, and delicate, while the man of taste appeared overly refined, if not actually affected.

Until the revolution, women in France continued to wear artificially widened skirts that were stretched out over a basket structure of three hoops, with the top hoop pulling in the waist painfully. Although the hairstyles were elaborate, with hair often heavily powdered, fashions in both hair and wigs changed rapidly when Queen Marie-Antoinette set a trend for a natural style; this fashion immediately sparked a craze for all sort of hats, from the coyest bonnet to the grandest of straw creations.

English women, meanwhile, wore rather "masculine" clothes; short jackets pushed out at the back by a bustle under skirts, tight bodices, and full, although not hooped, skirts were all common.

Men wore silk stockings, breeches, shirts tied at the collar with a scarf, waistcoats, and light overcoats. The waistcoat sometimes extended down to the knee, while the overcoat, no more than a long jacket, was tight across the chest, wide at the bottom, and slit in the back. The common style of hat was the three-cornered hat, worn even by women in Venice.

With the start of the French Revolution, silks and brocades were replaced by the "equality dress" of the common people. Shops selling reasonably priced ready-made clothes first appeared in Paris, the capital of fashion. The advent of such clothes created unemployment for many, as well as the loss of a number of traditional skills. The trend for ready-made clothes was one of the reasons for the new *neoclassical* look which came into fashion under Napoleon.

Although the middle classes followed aristocratic fashions, they didn't indulge in the lavish materials and flamboyant hairstyles of the rich, even when they could afford it. Indeed, those huge wigs and powdered pigtails gathered in a bow at the back of the neck were highly criticized, and the word queue ("pigtail") came to refer to a reactionary.

Except for their bright colors and braid, military uniforms were similar to the clothes of middle class men. Now, however, boots, which had been common in the seventeenth century, were no longer convenient for civilian use and were replaced by low court shoes with buckles. Women's shoes, decorated with delicate and costly embroidery, became increasingly elegant.

Hoopskirts were often cumbersome. The hoops themselves became oval in shape and wider at the sides, and women could then pass through doors or get into a coach sideways.

In the eighteenth century, the design of wooden sailing ships achieved near perfection. Although the armed vessels of the British East India Company were the finest ships afloat, there were few discernible differences in any of the ships of the various European countries. Around 1700, the helm became a wheel rather than a tiller, which gave greater precision in steering and lessened the risk of losing control during sudden gusts of wind. Best-known of all the English ships in service during the eighteenth century was the *Victory*, which mounted 102 cannon and sailed with a crew of 850. It was from this ship that Admiral Horatio Nelson directed the defeat of Napoleon's Franco-Spanish fleet at Trafalgar in 1805.

Roads were still appallingly bad. Travelers could go only a few dozen miles a day at most and transporting goods overland increased the final cost enormously. The need for improvements led to studies and experiments that eventually brought about changes in modern road-building techniques. France built a network of major arterial roads that converged in Paris, while other European countries undertook similar projects. To finance the construction and maintenance of roads, England revived the toll system whereby travelers had to pay in order to pass through gates in the road. Although these new or improved roads allowed for the establishment of efficient postal services as well as passenger services that used comfortable, sprung coaches, a long journey was still an adventure—and not always a pleasant one!

Early experimental private steam vehicles also ventured out on the new roads, but they were charged such high tolls that the experiments were soon abandoned; they were not to be resumed until decades later, on another type of road—the railroad.

Sailing ships that braved ocean crossings carried a spread of sails that made the vessels safer and easier to handle.

On new networks of roads, regular
public transportation services came
into being.

At the end of the eighteenth century, man
came close to achieving one of his most
ancient desires, flying, when the first
passengers rose up in a "boat" suspended
from a balloon and hovered in the air above
Paris for more than twenty minutes.

Among the first steam-powered vehicles was Nicolas
Joseph Cugnot's road wagon, introduced in 1769; it
ran at three miles per hour and could carry four
passengers. Unfortunately, Cugnot didn't seem to
have much interest in brakes; during a test drive, the
vehicle hit a wall and was damaged beyond repair.

111

The steam engine, which heralded the beginning of the Industrial Revolution, was undoubtedly the most important invention of the eighteenth century. At last mankind had at its disposal a means of converting heat energy into mechanical energy, a supply of energy that was dependent on neither wind nor water, as mills had been; that could be transported to where it was needed; and that required a form of energy, such as coal, that was available practically everywhere. Water was heated in a cylinder to create a head of steam pressure which in turn pushed a movable element within the cylinder, releasing energy that could run every conceivable kind of machine.

Equally important for industry were the advances in chemistry: a better understanding of the structure of matter and its various component elements, and of the laws governing the way elements are combined in different substances was achieved. Traditional alchemy, which had been purely practical, had also been highly mystical and not very exact. Now, observation of the various processes that matter undergoes enabled chemists to reproduce them, at least in part, so that a variety of products such as dyes, solvents, fertilizers, and detergents gradually became available for use in industry.

One indirect result of this chemical research was the discovery of a startling new form of energy, electricity. Although electricity was familiar as a natural phenomenon, it was not until the invention of batteries that it could at last be harnessed. Batteries consisted of a number of alternating copper and zinc sheets with an acid solution between them. The resulting movement of electrons from one pole of the battery to the other produced an electrical charge, a source of usable heat or energy.

In the field of optics, microscopes, which revealed a fantastic world of microorganisms within an ordinary drop of water or blood, were refined further, and medicine at last began its fight against infectious diseases.

The hydraulic pump, known as "the miner's friend," was powered by a steam engine. The piston movement, transmitted to the arm of the pump, pumped water out of mines continuously.

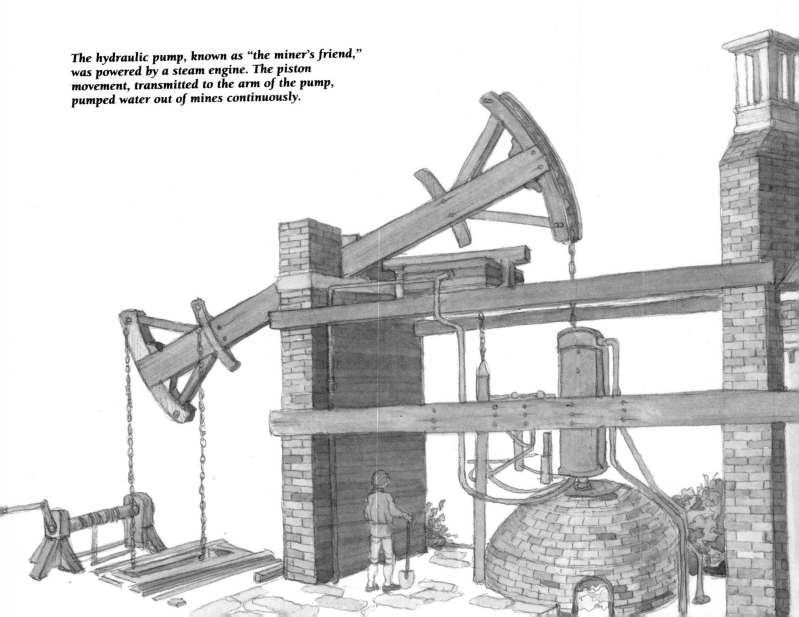

Coaches now had springs for a more comfortable ride.

Allesandro Volta's battery (1800)

Robert Hooke's microscope (17th century)

Bearings and suspension made coach travel comfortable at last. Mechanization, which became at once an obsession, a religion, and a game, even saw the invention of a mechanical duck (see below) with a digestive system!

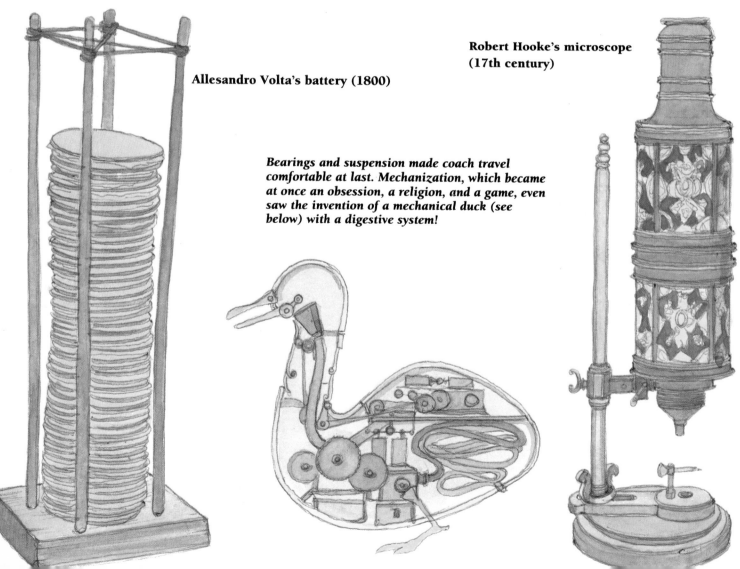

The eighteenth century began with the War of the Spanish Succession and ended with the early Napoleonic campaigns, and in between, bitter wars were fought over the succession to the Polish and Austrian thrones. Armies thus remained constantly mobilized.

As firearms evolved and became more effective, new tactical thinking was needed. The cavalry temporarily lost its importance, at least until rear-loading guns and pistols with automatic firing mechanisms were invented. Heavy cannon were now mounted only on ships, while on land campaigns, the more maneuverable models with more accurate sightings were used to zero in on specific targets rather than simply batter holes in walls. Battle lines, however, were still drawn up close together so that bullets continued to inflict damage.

All the great European armies introduced an elite cavalry corps of hussars, fighting men who, like the original hussar corps of Hungary, were held in awe for their bravery and ruthlessness in action. Sabreurs, cavalrymen who carried sabers, favored surprise charges; they often proved the decisive factor in a battle. Although armorers learned how to make bulletproof armor, it proved useless against artillery and so was abandoned during this period.

A French drummer and musketeer

Prussian artillerymen

A field cannon

Prussian grenadiers wearing typical headgear, similar to that of British grenadiers

Frederick II of Prussia's tallest and strongest soldiers were selected to become grenadiers, so named because they were armed with hand grenades. The soldier first lit the fuse of the gunpowder-packed grenade and then hurled it a great distance, and it would explode. After a time, such hand grenades fell into disuse, although they made a comeback in recent wars.

In hussar regiments, a man and his horse formed an inseparable unit. The hussars wore an "international" uniform that was virtually the same in all armies, with minor variations. The fur jerkin slung over the left shoulder would act as a shield for the least protected part of the body.

The Age of Progress

In 1815, the major powers of Europe convened at the Congress of Vienna in an effort to restore equilibrium among the European states. They attempted to remove the defeated Napoleon from circulation, as well as eradicate the memory of the French Revolution. However, under the pressure of liberal ideas and the more progressive members of the bourgeoisie, nearly all nineteenth-century European monarchs had to accept the participation of freely elected representatives of the new social forces in their governments. Not only did these liberal forces fight to bring about unified nations whose people shared a common ethnic, linguistic, and cultural background, but they also fought for freedom from the yoke of foreign powers.

Thus, in this century Italy and Germany both became united countries, Greece shook off Ottoman domination, and Czechs and Poles agitated to become independent nations. Small but active groups developed more advanced ideas about forms of republican and democratic governments, egalitarian and communist societies, and even anarchism. Although some political agitators succeeded in publicizing their ideas, they also ran the risk of imprisonment or exile because of their acts of terrorism.

Taking their cue from industrial developments in Great Britain, the rest of Europe and the United States rapidly turned to mechanized means of production. With an almost unlimited faith in the possibilities of technological progress, investors poured the capital that had accumulated in agricultural businesses and colonial trade into industry.

Urbanization—the shift of population from the country to the cities and towns—was another phenomenon that occurred to some extent in every country. The most heavily industrialized cities grew rapidly; their skylines, once dominated by cathedrals and government buildings, now bristled with factory chimneys. In France it was estimated that for every ten people living in the country, one lived in town, while in England, where industrialization had started fifty years earlier, the proportion of urban dwellers was twice as high.

Another factor in this shift of population was the availability of new and rapid means of transportation, particularly the railroad.

The constitutional monarchy

Parliament and the magistrature

The clergy

The national army

The enterprising middle class

The ideological revolutionary

At first the working classes objected to being herded together in the factories and down in the mines, and they protested violently against mechanization. In the end, however, they had to accept the harsh discipline of working under difficult conditions.

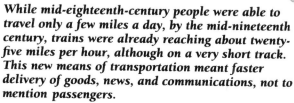

While mid-eighteenth-century people were able to travel only a few miles a day, by the mid-nineteenth century, trains were already reaching about twenty-five miles per hour, although on a very short track. This new means of transportation meant faster delivery of goods, news, and communications, not to mention passengers.

117

During the industrial era, major cities in northern Europe and the United States changed dramatically. Industrial zones and new residential areas sprawled around the old city centers, and railway stations were linked to the old quarters by broad avenues. In order to avoid the overcrowding and lack of facilities that made living in older areas so difficult, streets and even whole districts were demolished and rebuilt.

The middle classes who chose to live in open areas close to the center of the city built large private houses set in spacious gardens, while roads were built around the city walls to keep heavy traffic out of the center. In the heart of the city, with its congestion of carriages and pedestrians, streetcars drawn by horses made their way along iron tracks.

Public hygiene became important; complex sewage systems were constructed, drinking water was piped directly to houses through lead (and later, steel) pipes, and large cemeteries were built outside the cities. The most ambitious example of urban transformation in the nineteenth century was the design and building of the great boulevards in Paris.

The dominant architectural style was *neoclassicism,* which could be seen in huge and impressive residential blocks. Toward the end of the century, a more elaborate decorative style, *art nouveau,* appeared, while at the same time the building trade introduced new techniques for using steel and reinforced concrete.

The middle-class private house was large and functional, well heated, well lit, and easy to clean. Economical white-enameled iron stoves with a chimney tube for the smoke and a hood to catch the steam were placed in old fireplaces. Iceboxes replaced smelly larders, while adjustable oil lamps provided light, large stoves gave off heat, and copper tubs and a boiler heated water in the newest room in the house, the bathroom.

The gap between rich and poor was only too clearly demonstrated by the difference between their respective living conditions, with the common people, now called the *proletariat,* living in old tumbledown areas that backed onto the new avenues, or in sordid, smoke-clogged suburbs around the factories. The miserable living conditions of the workers became a chief concern of the socialists, as well as an important part of their political platform.

Country families, whether small landowners or tenants, lived in houses that hardly changed for centuries. There was a kitchen, called "the house," as that was where most activities took place, and a bedroom where parents and children slept together. In a stable either under the house or next to it were the animals, all of which had names. Many years had to pass before this kind of house included some of the space and comforts of the middle-class home. Day laborers who worked on the farms lived under even worse conditions.

Because main streets were at last lit by gas lamps tended by a lamplighter, people could now walk about safely outside at night. Roadsweepers kept the streets clean, and now that it was possible to hire cabs and use public transportation, it was no longer necessary to own a coach and horses.

Improvements in farming, which developed in the Netherlands and England and spread throughout Europe, were important not only to landowners and those who worked on the land, but to the state as well. The sweeping changes in land ownership that followed the French Revolution benefited both agriculture and the farmer, and the Napoleonic Wars destroyed once and for all the hierarchy of glebe peasantry that still survived in eastern Europe.

Although serfdom was abolished in 1861 in Russia, farming communities remained in a state of semi-serfdom for the entire nineteenth century. Meanwhile, in the United States, slavery continued to flourish on large plantations in the South, and it was not to be abolished formally until 1863.

Mechanization drew many workers from the land, as farming itself now began to be mechanized; this either shortened manpower hours on a job or did away with the job altogether. On the great farmlands of America, huge, newly invented steam-powered threshing machines attached to early mechanical harvesters did the work of many men.

Advances in chemistry improved methods of treating and preserving food. Sugar could now be extracted from the sugar beet, and so that crop was now grown almost everywhere.

Far from the stress of urban life, with only his own resources to rely on, the American farmer labored long and hard to achieve something permanent for himself and his family. However poor or inadequate, his farm or ranch was his own, although his striving for personal freedom in a new land often meant starting all over again under difficult circumstances.

The first canned food

Cattle brands

Limitless horizons opened up for the pioneer settlers in the American West; vast tracts of land were theirs to tame and cultivate. Cowboys, always in the saddle and sleeping under the stars, led a strenuous and lonely life, watching over and driving their herds of cattle.

121

Although new investment in equipment was constantly needed to keep up with the latest technology, industry proved to be highly profitable from the very beginning. Consequently, new production methods spread rapidly in northern Europe and the United States, while in more depressed areas, such as Italy, industrialization didn't really get under way until the twentieth century, and even then only in certain areas.

Despite the universal use of steam power, human labor was still the major form of energy in the new factories that continued to spring up in industrial cities. The new myth of progress dictated that production had to be ever greater and better, competitors had to be defeated, and markets captured. First and foremost, however, it was the profit motive that controlled production, and those who had to sweat and toil to produce for others the wealth they never enjoyed themselves felt constantly exploited. In order to protect their rights and negotiate wage contracts, these workers began to organize themselves into *trade unions*.

With little dignity attached to production-line work, people no longer had to master a trade, learn the secrets of a skill, or become specialists in their craft. Simple physical motions were often enough and even when precision work was occasionally needed for certain jobs, the worker had no sense of pride or achievement in the end product.

Nevertheless, handmade goods, produced with care to individual specifications, will always be preferred to mass-produced goods; thus, the traditional artisan has not vanished entirely, although since few people can afford such luxuries the number of professional craftsmen continues to decline. In an attempt to recover some of the traditional values, and in defiance of large-scale industry, William Morris promoted the Arts and Crafts movement in nineteenth-century England. Selecting and exhibiting work and designs in the applied arts, he strongly influenced subsequent notions of taste.

Because some of the wealth acquired through increased production went to finance new transportation routes such as roads and railways, rural improvements such as canals and irrigation systems, and new public administration buildings, industrial progress also benefited the public. Such projects took years to complete and employed large numbers of skilled and unskilled workers.

Depending on the quantity of carbon in iron, it can be soft iron or cast iron, or it can be made into steel. Steel, the most flexible, is the best-suited for sheeting; cast iron is hard but fragile; and soft iron, though very malleable, weakens quickly. Special blast furnaces were designed to extract carbon from iron; here we see a huge steam-powered hammer for working steel.

These children are not going to school, but to work in a factory or a mine.

Although the colonies still supplied raw materials for European industry, mechanization meant that European-produced goods became competitive with those produced in the colonies. Commerce in exotic goods was still a thriving business. Coffee and cocoa became increasingly popular, especially when it was discovered that roasting the beans improved the flavor.

It took generations for a new image of the sailor to evolve and for shipyards to change; steam-powered ships were still in their infancy in the nineteenth century. Sailing ships, with metal hulls and masts, tapering forms, ever larger sails, and more sophisticated rigging devices, were remarkably efficient and could stay at sea for long stretches of time under all sorts of conditions.

In the hopes of finding their fortunes, people from all walks of life traveled to the most remote areas of the American continent to find gold. As it turned out, these gold prospectors were the vanguard of a great migration which in a few decades saw the United States stretching from the Appalachian Mountains to the Rockies and from there to the Pacific. This expanding nation not only developed a vast independent trade base, but also quickly became competitive with Europe and Great Britain so that by the end of the nineteenth century, the United States had developed into the world's first fully industrialized nation.

In contrast, outside powers still had considerable control in Latin America, and although the major countries had attained formal independence, their resources were exploited so seriously that any industrial or commercial growth they might have developed on their own was seriously undermined.

Gold prospectors

Tea was an important commodity, not only because it was so widely used, but also because it engendered such large profit margins for its importers.

From the very beginning, the United States had a sound economic structure headed by bold managers and entrepreneurs who welcomed new technology and were farsighted in their investments. Loyalty to their country and a sense of breaking new frontiers, both physical and economic, were predominant traits of the American character.

Raw cotton from the United States was exported to Europe, where newly mechanized spinning and weaving factories worked it into cloth.

The most perfect sailing ship ever designed was the American clipper.

125

The very tailors and dressmakers who had enjoyed aristocratic patronage before the French Revolution were now designing new styles. Attempts to reintroduce the fashions of the past after the Congress of Vienna in 1815 all failed. Instead, the Romantic woman was expected to look and act like the heroines of contemporary literature, who were pale, languid, sensitive, and prone to tears.

Narrow waists returned, with billowing skirts concealing layers of petticoats which in turn were soon replaced by the crinoline, an underskirt of horsehair or stiff cotton that stretched out the full, light-textured skirt above. Next came the half-crinoline; with it only the lower part of the skirt was puffed out, and the material at the top of the skirt was gathered over padding at the small of the back so that the skirt hung down in broad swaths. At this time a much-abused group of eccentric women, the "lionesses," followed the example of the celebrated female writer George Sand who often wore male attire to match her nom de plume.

Men's fashions took their lead from England, where Beau Brummel, the greatest dandy of the age, defined elegance as the quality of always being dressed perfectly for any function at any time of day so that one would not be noticed. Breeches, which were usually a different color and material from the jacket, became longer and were buttoned down the front rather than at the sides. Until the appearance of the elegant tailcoat, which was cut away at the waist with the tail flaps hanging behind, jackets were quite long. In direct contrast to the earlier fashion for wigs, hair was now worn very short, although shoulder-length hair was still acceptable. Top hats were the norm for headgear. Shirts, with upturned collars, were worn with cravats of fine material which were knotted and bowed in various styles.

For women, dressing was an
elaborate process. Preparing
for a reception or ball was an
especially time-consuming task
that usually required the
assistance of at least one maid.
The style of dress depended on
the occasion: a broad-collared
dress and shawl would be worn
in the afternoon; a cape was
worn over the dress for
shopping; evening wear was
décolleté; and modest but
beautiful informal attire was
suitable at-home wear.

Revolutionary improvements in transportation took place during the age of coal and steel, with the development of steam-powered ships and trains around the middle of the nineteenth century undoubtedly the most dramatic. Although the early iron ships built at the beginning of the century had been replaced by steel liners, the use of steam as a means of propulsion still presented problems, and naval engineers concentrated throughout the century on the possibilities of either paddle wheels or propellers. Experiments finally proved that propellers completely immersed in the water provided the most efficient means of steam-powered propulsion.

Iron rails had already been used successfully in the mines, where they served as rails for trolley cars, replacing the old wooden tracks. They also proved to be durable when installed in city streets for horse-drawn trams, the disadvantage being that the trams were then limited to the route of the tracks.

Although it was little more than a demonstration model, the Catch Me Who Can, the first locomotive to pull a passenger train, appeared in 1808. Among the world's early public railways to open was the Liverpool–Manchester line in 1830. It was the first to rely completely on locomotive power. Within decades, rail networks expanded everywhere, becoming increasingly faster and making better connections so that rail travel became the vogue for holidays, especially to the mountains and the seashore, leaving coach travel for those places where the railroad had not yet reached. By the end of the century, steam locomotives had already begun to be replaced by electric ones.

A transatlantic paddle steamer

A steam locomotive

The German inventor Otto Lilienthal, who successfully flew in a machine heavier than air, might be considered the true pioneer of modern flying. He built a whole series of flying machines, both monoplanes and biplanes, as well as gliders designed to be launched from hilltops. Lilienthal made over a thousand flights before a fatal crash in 1896.

A horse-drawn trolley

A stagecoach

Although steam was used more and more successfully, toward the end of the nineteenth century a new internal combustion engine was developed which eliminated the need for a cumbersome boiler and a stock of coal. Energy was produced by a piston in a cylinder, which was pushed by an explosion of air and combustible gas, ignited by a spark. Later, for great power, the air-and-gas mixture was made to explode when compressed by the piston after it had sucked the mixture in; thus, the four-stroke engine (suction, compression, explosion, expulsion) was born. Gasoline now became the main fuel.

Not only was this kind of engine more efficient, but it could also be used in small private vehicles. Since the recent invention of bicycles showed how much people enjoyed moving about freely by mechanical means, the transition to motorcycles and automobiles was rapid.

Now that the old problem of rear-loading was solved, remarkable progress was also made with firearms. With the invention of a movable mechanism that allowed the bullet charge to be set in place at the back of the barrel, and a firing device that set off the charge automatically, ramrods, wadding, and fuses were no longer necessary.

Electric batteries, which provided a continuous current, also provided the impetus for many inventions, most notably the telegraph and the light bulb.

The telegraph took advantage of the discovery of the electromagnetic effects of electrical current. Other effects of electrical current were used in the voltaic arc and in the filament light bulb; in the latter, thermal effects were exploited, with high-resistance conductors being heated white-hot.

The first signal transmitted long-distance by cable with Saemmering's "telephone" was acoustical. Samuel Morse, who developed the Morse code used today, built the electro-magnetic recording telegraph illustrated at right.

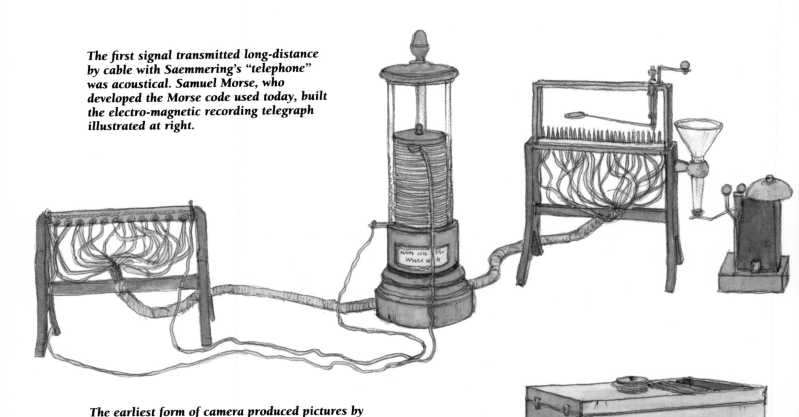

The earliest form of camera produced pictures by means of glass covered with light-sensitive silver salts.

George Stephenson's steam locomotives first demonstrated the potential of railroads, a means of transportation that spread rapidly throughout nineteenth-century Europe.

Colt, Remington, and Smith & Wesson were famous names everywhere. These American revolvers and rifles were the first automatic weapons with rotating chambers.

By 1866 America and Europe were already linked by underwater telegraphic cable.

For over twenty years after the French Revolution, a coalition of European states was pitted against the military genius of Napoleon, whose brilliant campaigns took him to the very heart of Russia. Welcomed and admired by the libertarians and democrats of the countries he invaded, he soon began to show a thirst for power that Austria, England, and Prussia were determined to check at all costs.

In some of the most celebrated battles in history, Napoleon's armies experienced exhilarating victories in Italy and Germany, dreadful suffering during the midwinter retreat from Russia, bitter defeat at Leipzig, and the disillusionment of a complete rout at Waterloo.

At one time serious wounds on the battlefield were "treated" by amputation, also known as the *coup de grâce,* or mercy stroke. Now the wagons accompanying the armies also included an "ambulance" for carrying the wounded quickly to a field hospital where bleeding could be stopped and infections dealt with, although amputation was still often necessary.

Napoleonic soldiers

Guns had bayonets fixed on the end for use at a distance and at close quarters, thus providing the soldier with a two-in-one weapon.

Soldiers like the one on the left fought in the American Civil War.

An ambulance

The infantry of the anti-Napoleonic coalition

French grenadiers

Cartridge case, shot, and cartridges

English infantrymen

133

Two major phenomena are important in understanding twentieth-century prosperity: the concentration of the population in cities, and the distribution of the labor force in three areas—agriculture, industry, and trade and public services.

Although the situation in what is now called the Third World was quite different, urbanization was a clear indication of the economic development of the industrialized countries. With the exception of ancient Rome, no European city had more than a million inhabitants before 1750, and only two, London and Paris, had over half a million. Prior to the Industrial Revolution, urban communities accounted for less than twenty percent of the population, while this rose to forty percent at the turn of the twentieth century (the urban population is about seventy percent at the present time, and eighty percent is forecast by the year 2000). Meanwhile, about fifty cities had grown to a million inhabitants, with Paris and London now both vast metropolises.

The shift of population from the countryside to towns and cities meant that fewer and fewer people produced the food necessary to sustain society. On the one hand, the population was growing, while on the other, with increased productivity of the land and mechanization of labor, less manpower was required to feed everybody. Workers now turned to other areas of employment, which in turn increased overall national productivity and prosperity.

At one time farm workers formed the bulk of the labor force. This situation changed dramatically with the onset of the Industrial Revolution and the urbanization that followed. At the beginning of the twentieth century, about half the active population of industrialized countries worked the land. These numbers dropped even lower in recent years—in the United States, for instance, to about only three percent.

In contrast, the percentage of workers in industry has only recently begun to level out. In fact, the percentage has begun to decline as industry has become saturated with an excess work force, just as agriculture had an excess work force in the past. In the area of trade and public service, there has been an enormous upswing, so that the number of people now employed in clerical, technical, managerial, and academic jobs not directly concerned with production exceeds that of people in industry, and the gap continues to widen.

RUSSIA

1 person in 20 lived in cities

Industry

Commerce and services

Agriculture

FRANCE

2 people in 20 lived in cities

Industry

Commerce and services

Agriculture

GREAT BRITAIN

UNITED STATES

4 people in 20
lived in cities

5 people in 20
lived in cities

Industry

Commerce and services

Industry

Commerce and services

Agriculture

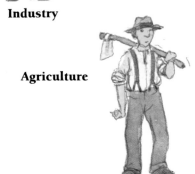

Agriculture

New building materials, including steel and reinforced concrete, opened up many opportunities for architects and engineers at the end of the nineteenth century. After World War I, in both Europe and America, strict functionalism became the order of the day. The trend was to get away from traditional styles, to unleash the imagination in the quest for fresh forms, to make the most of the technological possibilities of new building materials.

Even in the most futuristic skyscraper, living space was planned according to everyday requirements of the family, with no space going unused. Every dwelling now had features that were previously unknown—electric lights, gas, central heating, a refrigerator, bathrooms with hot and cold running water, and all sorts of labor-saving electrical devices such as vacuum cleaners and washing machines. Home communications were radically altered by the advent of the telephone, radio, and, ultimately, television.

Just as production of these appliances requires a huge labor force, so running and maintaining a modern city takes a vast amount of work. Think of what lies below the streets of Paris or New York, or for that matter imagine how much technology is needed to provide necessary services even to small towns.

During World War I, a war that changed Old World ways once and for all, the most gifted European and American architects were already sketching out the new shapes of the future. Reason and imagination united to plan how best to use the new industrial technology without either impersonal "design" or financial considerations becoming the controlling factor. Furniture, now mass-produced, also became simpler and more functional, although designers retained a fondness for good materials as well as unique and special touches.

**Einstein Tower,
Potsdam, Germany (1919)**

New home comforts

The Empire State Building was built between 1930 and 1932. Its 1,472 feet (including transmitting tower) made it the tallest building in the world for a long time.

Modern agriculture, whose main goals are maximum productivity per acre and mechanization of farming techniques, has seen its work force dwindle more and more as time goes on. In order to produce more food for less cost, farmers have cultivated the most fertile areas intensively and abandoned less productive areas where for centuries peasants made their livelihood. Research into fertilizers and irrigation has increased output sometimes as much as tenfold.

At the same time, neglect of mountain areas created, and still creates, serious hydro-geological problems. The hilly land around the Mediterranean, ideal for grapevines and olive trees, has had to be cultivated carefully to make the use of machinery possible, and this work is now beginning to pay off.

On more level ground, plowing with the tractor, that symbol of modern farming, has allowed maximum use of the top layer of soil. Tractors, used for a hundred and one different jobs—pulling, pumping water from wells, driving other machines such as threshers, and so on— are only one kind of agricultural machine that has been developed to make farm work easier and faster.

Nitrogen- and potassium-based fertilizers are used to enrich heavily farmed land, while various chemicals minimize the ravages of insects and microorganisms; however, these chemicals are poisonous and must be used with caution.

A tractor

138

Drawn by horses or oxen, the earliest harvesting machine had wheels that turned the axle, which was attached to the blades.

Aerial crop-spraying

A disk harrow

By the beginning of the twentieth century, many machines were already powered by electric or internal combustion engines. Nobody worried about oil or gas reserves, nor did anybody anticipate the problem of pollution caused by fuel-powered machinery and vehicles. Electricity was produced mainly by hydroelectric power stations; efficient distribution of this clean energy made it possible to set up industrial plants in almost any location.

Workshops and factories became completely mechanized. The work was divided into individual jobs and each job was assigned to a certain group of workers. Although a degree of skill was still required, especially in the manufacture of luxury goods, where workers could feel pride in their part of the process, most plants required assembly-line work. Now workers mechanically performed the same operation over and over, day in and day out, and the finished product was seemingly unrelated to any one individual's work.

On the other hand, this was the only way goods could be produced cheaply enough to be made available to everyone, so that although work itself was less satisfying, there was the satisfaction of increased buying power. Now, with the help of the mysterious forces of advertising, which whets the appetite for luxuries as well as necessities, ours has become a consumer society.

Even today, skilled or semiskilled labor is still needed in such industries as the building trade, where prefabrication and assembly-line methods aren't generally used. As a result, houses are extremely expensive in relation to other commodities, such as mass-produced cars.

Not only was manual labor necessary to industry, but mental labor was essential as well, exemplified by a whole new work force of technicians and administrators. The development of automation techniques, such as the use of computers, has reduced the need for manpower even more.

The automobile industry

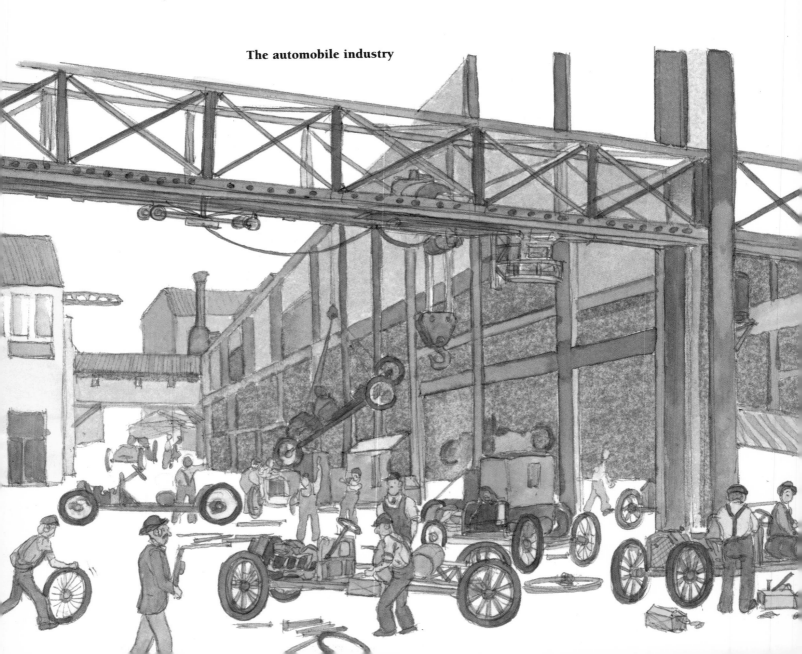

Because photographic enlargement processes had not yet been perfected, a giant camera was designed to produce a giant photograph of the joining of the two sections of the transcontinental railroad in Utah.

An oil refinery

As use of the internal combustion engine increased, oil became a vital source of energy, representing five percent of total energy consumption at the start of this century and twenty percent by the 1930s. At this time natural gas began to be tapped, not so much for power as for heat.

Europe, which depended entirely on African and Middle Eastern countries for its oil, made many of these countries into colonies or dominions, using European capital to build wells there. Most tankers carrying oil to Europe came from the Arab world, making the Suez Canal of strategic importance.

The development of merchant shipping throughout the century has been enormous, starting with the universal switch to steam. With steamship tonnage increasing tenfold, the Atlantic crossing became safer and more comfortable, and took only half the time. Such improvements helped to encourage a new wave of immigration to the United States.

Forty years after the first railway line was laid, Europe had over 55,000 miles of track, with almost the same distance of track in both the United States and Canada. By the first decade of the twentieth century, the figure had risen considerably.

The improvement in the various means of transportation went hand in hand with the development of international trade, which tripled in volume between 1870 and 1913. Throughout the nineteenth century, the bulk of world trade had been under British control, but by the beginning of World War I, the United States, France, and Germany had become close competitors. London, however, remained the hub of the complex exchange system and the center of international banking.

In the year after the Suez Canal opened in 1869, 437,000 tons of goods passed through its locks. By 1913, the year before World War I, this figure had risen to over 20 million.

The drilling and commercial use of oil gave birth to the petrochemical industry, which not only converted crude oil into fuel, but also introduced by-products such as plastics and synthetic fibers.

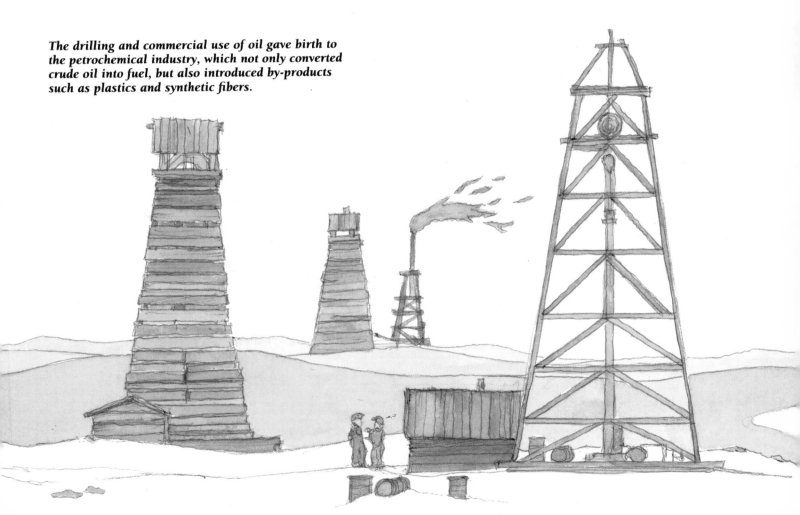

The *art nouveau* mood of the turn of the century was the final florid, fanciful fling of traditional styles in dress. Full of lighthearted gaiety and confidence in the new century, the appropriately named *belle époque* saw its stage and music-hall stars often dictating fashion.

Early-twentieth-century fashions were still nineteenth-century in tone, although an occasional ankle appeared and some of the great floating swaths of material were trimmed down. Actually, "twentieth-century fashions" didn't really begin until after World War I; this war marked the end of an era and the beginning of modernity. The knee-length skirts worn with necklaces dangling to the knees that appeared in the Roaring Twenties would have been scandalous earlier, while Coco Chanel's "simple and extremely expensive" outfits would have seemed unnecessarily severe.

At the beginning of the century, men, with their black tailcoats and bowlers or top hats, seemed to be permanently in mourning. Their overcoats, however, made of a variety of materials and colors, showed more imagination. The entrepreneurial and mercantile bourgeoisie presented an austere, frugal image; the sober quality of their clothes suggested their solid bank balances. The ideal *belle epoque* male was tall and well built, with a moustache and beard, or at least a moustache. And then Mr. Gillette patented his razor blade . . .

Feminine accessories, which were many and elaborate, included bags, parasols, and huge hats with feathers and flowers. Male dandies were elaborately turned out too, with top hats, silver-knobbed canes, and silver cigarette cases. The children of the day dressed like miniature adults.

With the commercial development of the internal combustion engine, the great age of travel and transportation began. A wide variety of machines flooded the market, from two-wheel pedal vehicles with engines, which had appeared in the nineteenth century as mechanical curiosities, to the earliest motorized coaches of 1885, and then on to the exciting Fords and Alfa Romeos that appeared in the first decades of the twentieth century. A major innovation was the use of tires, thanks to developments in the rubber industry.

World War I provided powerful incentives for research involving both ships and flying machines. Battleships and submarines appeared on the war scene, but flight was the great adventure. Lighter-than-air gas balloons were built into rigid, aerodynamically designed frames that could be maneuvered easily and could even fly across the Atlantic.

Airplanes, which were faster and more maneuverable than balloons, developed so rapidly they became a formidable element in World War I. Because there were so few landing strips, for a long time in the early days of flight seaplanes were more popular than airplanes. After World War I, however, when the airplane's body was strengthened and light but powerful engines were mounted, airplanes began to be mass-produced. With these improvements, they became a reliable and, above all, useful means of transportation, capable of flying 120 miles per hour and of traveling some 600 miles per flight.

After World War I, the craze for record breaking began, the most famous achievement being Lindbergh's flight from New York to Paris in May, 1927. His accomplishment opened the possibility of regular air service between North America and Europe.

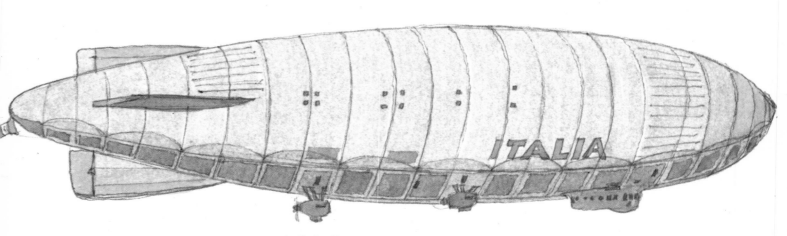

Best known of all airships were those built by Count Ferdinand Zeppelin in Germany and by General Umberto Nobile in Italy. After his dangerous but lucky expedition to the North Pole with the Norge in 1926, Nobile tried again two years later in the Italia. This second flight ended in failure when the airship broke up on the return voyage.

The first submarine was the Nautilus, built by the American inventor Robert Fulton at the beginning of the nineteenth century. By World War I, a century later, all the countries at war put submarines to military use.

During World War I, tens of thousands of flying machines were built. Their engines were similar to car engines, and they were constructed with common materials such as wood and oilskin, with steel tie-rods holding the structure together.

Cars built by Ford and Alfa Romeo, two of the first great car manufacturers.

Research into the induction of an electrical current with magnets led to the invention of the dynamo, which produced electricity, with alternators designed to provide an alternating current and transformers to increase the voltage or change the current. Only a high-voltage alternating current, in fact, can be carried by a conductor without considerable loss of energy. To make the rotors turn around the magnet, that is, to set the turbine going, oil-fueled internal combustion engines were used. The same procedure is still followed today in electric power stations, although on a much larger scale.

Another "fuel supply" for electrical power stations is water. The force of waterfalls can be harnessed to create mechanical energy, as has been done since long ago. The drawback is that the location of the power station is dictated by the location of an adequate water supply, while the current, in turn, has to be carried wherever it is needed, often at considerable expense. Nevertheless, this source of energy is inexhaustible, it creates no pollution, and it is free, once the initial construction costs have been covered.

Distribution of electric current for lighting requires a simple, easily manageable "receiver": either an arc lamp, such as that used in some film projectors; a filament bulb, which was originally invented by Thomas Edison in 1879; or a fluorescent bulb, which functions through the agitation of certain gases as the current passes through.

The conquest of the sky really began in 1903, with Orville and Wilbur Wright's first motor-powered flight on the coast of North Carolina. Tens of thousands of aircraft would be in the air only fifteen years later! Jet planes, which were invented in the forties, have now almost completely replaced the old propeller type.

One of the greatest and most spectacular achievements of our century has been the development of communication by means of electromagnetic waves. Guglielmo Marconi, who had already transmitted a radio signal in 1895, was experimenting with radar by 1926. Since after World War II, radios and televisions have been new sources for information and entertainment in the home, and although the quality of reception for each was not always perfect at first, both media were immediate successes. Science and technology have produced countless developments. Among them are advances in microbiology, which have given the world vaccines against numerous diseases, and the nuclear reactor, developed in 1942, which harnessed a new form of energy.

On December 17, 1903, with Orville Wright steering and his brother Wilbur running along behind, the first aircraft took off.

After the first models were produced by the German inventor Gottlieb Daimler, motorcycles quickly evolved into something very similar to what they are today, with air-cooled engines and chain drives.

The first radio broadcast of popular music after World War I marked the beginning of a new era in entertainment.

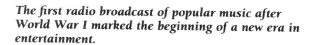

The famous transatlantic liner Titanic struck an iceberg on its maiden voyage and sank.

The formation of national states continued up until World War I. This was caused in part by economic problems and in part by Austria's and Germany's hunger for power; it resulted in several million lives lost, and even boys barely seventeen years old were sent to the front lines. Although in time older men were also drafted into the armed services, national armies were now made up of all male citizens around the age of twenty by means of a compulsory draft.

Although naval power had increased considerably and the air corps became a third armed force, the bulk of the vast national armies was still the infantry with all its various branches. The cavalry, meanwhile, disappeared altogether in favor of motorized vehicles, vans, jeeps, trucks, motorcycles, and armored tanks.

Battle techniques changed too. First aircraft would bombard enemy lines. Tanks and then infantry would follow, and heavy artillery provided backup fire.

Uniforms, helmets, and weapons differed little among the European armies.

A German infantryman and an Italian *alpino*

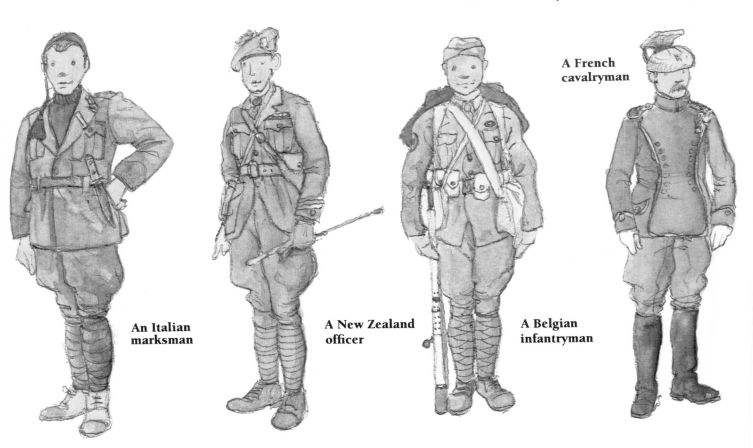

An Italian marksman

A New Zealand officer

A Belgian infantryman

A French cavalryman

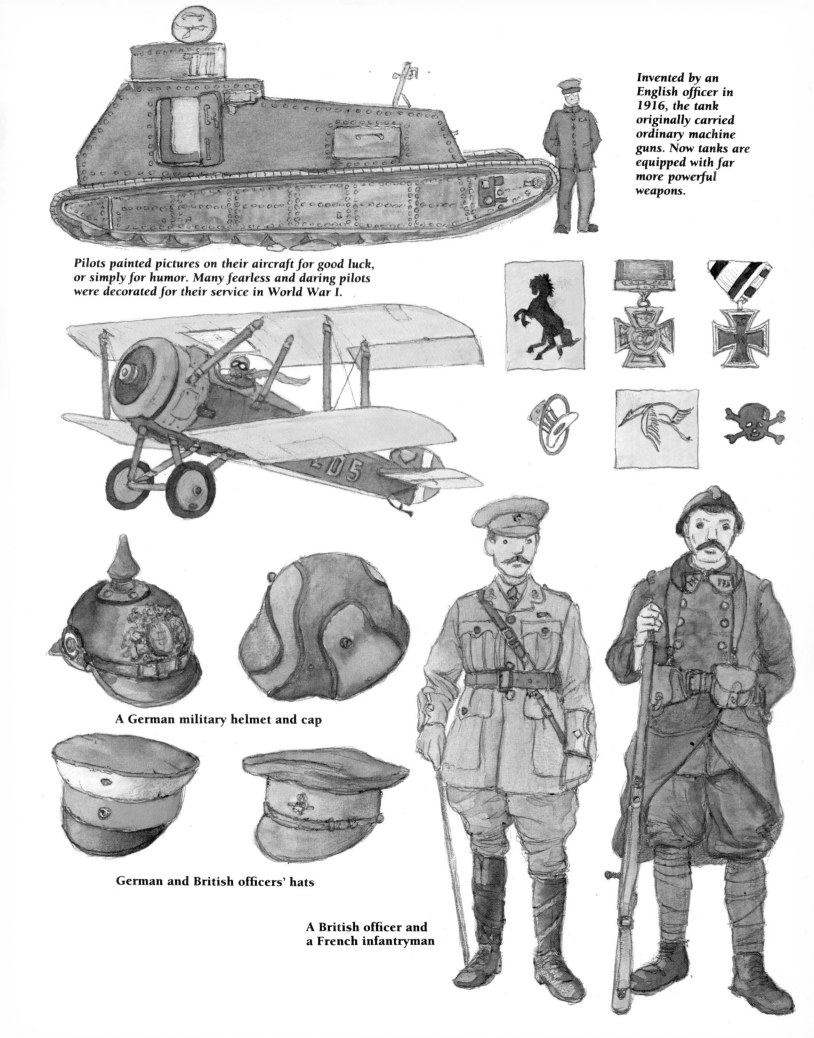

Invented by an English officer in 1916, the tank originally carried ordinary machine guns. Now tanks are equipped with far more powerful weapons.

Pilots painted pictures on their aircraft for good luck, or simply for humor. Many fearless and daring pilots were decorated for their service in World War I.

A German military helmet and cap

German and British officers' hats

A British officer and a French infantryman

Additional Information To The Chapters

The Ancient World

The period covered in this chapter extends from the dawn of history to the Hellenistic age, from the first signs of human civilization to the expansion of Greek influence in the countries around the Mediterranean. The Hellenistic period, in fact, followed the many conquests of Alexander the Great, who died in 323 B.C., leaving his empire to the generals who had helped create it. The emphasis in this section is on the period of most intense contact between the ancient civilizations, toward the end of the second millenium B.C. The Hittite empire then broke up, while Mesopotamia experienced a long succession of ruling dynasties, starting with the Sumerians and ending with the Persians; the latter emerged as a power in the second half of the first millennium B.C., concurrent with the growth of Greek cities. The civilization that left the greatest mark on the history of the Western world in terms of language, art, philosophy, and scientific thought was that of Greece. And of great importance to the development of Western religious and moral thought was Hebrew culture, which passed on to modern culture the religions of Judaism and Christianity.

Worship   In the world of the primitive nomad, worship was concentrated on the stars. The observation of the sky and its changes were fundamental in establishing the cycle of migrations. Ever since then, time has been measured by astronomical phenomena such as the rotation of the earth (day), the phases of the moon (weeks), the revolution of the moon (month), the equinoxes and solstices (seasons), and the revolution of the earth (year). This rhythm is still marked by holidays such as Sunday and New Year's.

When once— nomadic tribes became settled and their interests turned to working the land, worship began to center around the fertility of plants and animals. Mother Earth became the most important divinity. An almost inextricable mixture of the two great religious expressions, Earth and Sky, is to be found in Greek mythology, which is based on religious stories (myths) and practices (rites).

Burial   It seems certain that the earliest Mediterranean people buried their dead. After the invasions of Nordic peoples, however, cremation became predominant. The two types of funeral customs seem to imply two different primitive religious tendencies, one toward the earth as mother of all living things, to which every being returns after death, the other toward the sky, into which the smoke of the pyres rises, accompanying the spirit of the dead person.

Crops   The basic food of ancient people consisted of various types of grain: wheat, barley, oats, millet, sesame, all rich in proteins, vitamins, and oils. The farming of the ancient civilizations revolved very largely around these crops, whose greatest advantage was that they could be stored for a long time without spoiling. Fruit—particularly citrus fruit—was regarded as a luxury; only kings had orange groves.

Meat was eaten only after the entrails of the animal had been burned in honor of the gods. Various aromatic herbs were used to remove unpleasant cooking smells and thus make the offerings acceptable to the gods. This is the origin of cooking meat with rosemary, sage, bay leaves, and other sweet-smelling herbs, a custom which has been retained over the centuries.

Pottery   Terra-cotta is a basic clay, modeled and dried in special ovens. Fine white clay such as kaolin was later used, to make more delicate yet stronger ceramics such as porcelain, which is Chinese in origin.

Each historical period had its own style of decoration; a naturalistic style was typical of Crete and a geometric style was used in archaic Greece. The two best-known painting styles for Greek cermics are black-figured, in which figures are painted in black on a red background, and details are scratched in; and red-figured, in which red figures are painted on a black ground bordering the figure, to which various tiny details are added in black. These styles differ in a similar way to positive and negative images in photography.

Metals   After the Stone Age periods of ancient history are defined on the basis of the metals people used. There is first an Age of Copper; copper being a soft metal which is easy to smelt; then a Bronze Age, in which a knowledge of alloys was necessary, because bronze is made up of copper and tin; and finally an Iron Age, named for a metal which has a very high melting point and was therefore more difficult to obtain, but which is also much stronger than other metals. This system for dating and naming civilizations does not imply that other metals—lead, gold, and silver, for instance—were not known at the same time. These metals were relatively easy to smelt and work with, but some, such as gold, were also hard to find. Before the first mines were set up, gold was obtained from sandy riverbeds.

Glass   Glass was probably discovered when men saw that the sand over which metals were smelted dissolved on contact with the incandescent materials, giving a compact, semitransparent paste, which could be molded while it was hot. Glassmaking was highly developed in Syrian cities in the first few centuries B.C.; these very early workshops were already experimenting with the technique of glass-blowing, to obtain hollow containers such as vases and bottles.

Trade   The Cretans are mentioned on an Egyptian inscription of the New Kingdom as paying tributes to the pharaoh for many products. These were probably not actually tributes, but records of the trade the Cretans carried on throughout the Mediterranean. The Phoenicians were equally renowned as merchants and navigators. Besides the excellent purple dye they extracted from a shell, their national product was cedar wood, which they brought down from the mountains of Lebanon, and which was said to have been used in great quantities for Solomon's temple in Jerusalem.

Apart from trade, there were also cultural exchanges between peoples. Each year on the beaches of Byblos, a city in Phoenicia, the "head" of Osiris arrived over the waves. Osiris was the Egyptian god who, in myth, was killed and hacked to pieces by the demon Seth. The women of Byblos performed the ritual of carrying the head to the temple and would then begin a great celebration. The story has it that the goddess Isis through her love gave life to her lamented husband once again.

Cities   Modern excavations in Syrian cities such as Ugarit and Ebla give us a clear idea of the layout of ancient city-states. They had an acropolis, or "high city," the well-fortified site of the temple and palace; the people's dwellings were at the foot of the acropolis, set along streets and squares. Further down the hill the city was ringed and protected by another circle of walls.

Fabrics   The fabric most commonly used in Egypt was obtained from the fibers of flax, grown along the banks of the Nile. In Greece, most material was made from sheep's wool. Fibers were spun and twisted by hand by women in their homes. Both men and women have always been involved in the weaving and making of clothes.

Boats   We do not have any definite information on the Cretan and Phoenician fleets. But we do know, from the Greek historian Herodotus, that at the battle of Salamis (480 B.C.) the Persians attacked with a powerful fleet, while the Greeks (who won the battle) had a fleet of 378 ships. Earlier information about Greek ships can be found in the epic poems of Homer.

Roads   The greatest road builders of antiquity, before the Romans, were undoubtedly the Persians. The only really good Greek roads were those along processional routes, which led to great shrines, like the road from Athens to Eleusis. The custom of traveling a processional route to a shrine is followed even to this day, in the religious rite of pilgrimage.

Technology   In antiquity, technical knowledge, particularly that concerned with metalwork, was held in strict secrecy and regarded as a semi-divine skill. Greek mythology produced Prometheus, the demigod who tamed fire, and Hephaestus, the god who made weapons for heroes. In reality metals came from jealously guarded centers of production, and were traded either in ingots, like copper, or in ready-shaped objects, such as iron goods.

Writing   The interpretation of cuneiform and hieroglyphic writing became possible only when these systems were discovered in documents alongside a translation into at least one known language. The Rosetta stone, seized by the French during the Egyptian campaign led by Napoleon in 1798, provided the key to deciphering Egyptian hieroglyphics with matching texts in hieroglyphic, demotic, and Greek. Jean-Francois Champollion broke the code by comparing two known words: *Cleopatra* and *Ptolmis* (Ptolemy V, during whose reign the stone was inscribed). Both words contained *p* and *l*, letters which yielded corresponding hieroglyphs and consistent sounds.

Weapons   Societies condemn war only when the advantages of victory seem too slight in relation to losses and sacrifices. In antiquity the losses in human life seemed small indeed, compared to the very considerable booty to be gained. Furthermore, wars were decided mostly in combat between armies, without serious harm to the civilian population. A war chariot drawn by two horses could spread terror among the enemy ranks without doing very much damage. However, a man could die from a slight wound, since there were no medicines to prevent infection. Powerful infusions of herbs were used to lessen pain, but they could not necessarily save lives.

One Great Empire Alone

This chapter deals with the Roman Empire at the height of its power and expansion, around A.D. 100. The Roman Empire, established by Octavian Augustus at the end of the civil wars, in 26 B.C., lasted in the West until A.D. 476, when the last emperor, Romulus Augustulus, was deposed. The emperor Trajan (A.D. 98-117) carried out a series of military campaigns to extend and stabilize the borders of the empire to the north and east. His exploits are immortalized in the bas-reliefs of Trajan's Column, erected in his honor in Rome. With his successor, Hadrian, came a time of peace and prosperity throughout the regions administered by the Romans.

Cities   The cities founded or taken over by the Romans had a sense of order not only due to functional considerations, but also based on ancient religious rituals. Surveyors looked to augurs for help in establishing the center of the city, where the two main axes would cross. These soothsayers performed propitiation rites and watched for omens that would direct them, such as the flight of birds. Rome itself was thought to have been founded on a sacred act.

Architecture and the Figurative Arts   Many scholars talk about the Romans' eclecticism in art, that is, their ability to take ideas and techniques from various different artistic traditions, such as the Greek and Etruscan. They nonetheless developed certain building types and stylistic innovations on their own. The ampitheater, basilica, and baths are buildings with no exact equivalent in other civilizations, and the fondness for rounded forms such as the arch, cylinder, and dome is typically Roman. In sculpture and painting too the Romans introduced a new element, realism, in contrast to the earlier Greeks who tended to idealize the human figure according to laws of perfection more suited to the representation of the gods than ordinary mortals.

Despite its monumental forms and decorations, Roman architecture was always functional. Referring to the aqueducts, a senator is said to have commented, "These are our pyramids."

Land Reclamation   When they founded their colonies, the Romans often chose marshy or barren land and carried out large-scale reclamation projects. Examples of these operations can be seen today in the Po Valley in Italy, at the mouth of the Rhone in France, and around Cambridge in England.

Public Works   Strict records were kept about the subdivision of urban land into building lots and of the countryside into cultivable plots. These records, etched on bronze tablets, were stored in Rome. Some lots were earmarked for the building of public facilities, including baths and lavatories. Sewage systems carried waste and dirty water from the city.

The Romans remained unsurpassed in public works and

road building. Most roads bore the names of the consul under whose jurisdiction they had been built: for example, the Via Aemilia, the Via Aurelia, the Via Cassia, and the Via Flaminia.

Lawmaking Laws also bore the name of the man who had drafted them, followed by a reference to the matter with which they dealt. Roman law is still studied today as the basis of modern law, because it represents a fine balance between respect for the freedom of the individual and the powers of public institutions.

The Army The wagons that accompanied the Roman legions with supplies, tools, and equipment were generally an easy prey for the enemy and slowed down the march. After Marius's reform of the military system in 100 B.C., legionnaires loaded themselves with all their personal baggage and carried it on their shoulders like a pack saddle. Legionnaires were thus known as "Marius's mules."

Camps were drawn up according to a precise plan, with the administrative buildings and the commander's house (that is, the general staff headquarters) in the center, and barracks at the sides. The defense works stood about twenty yards from the barracks, to avoid being struck by missiles thrown from outside.

The legion was held together by iron discipline; rewards for victory were considerable, but punishment for any violation was extremely severe. Anyone turning tail before the enemy was whipped until blood flowed, and capital punishment was meted out to deserters. The legion's banner was never allowed to leave the camp, while the banner of the maniple represented the unifying spirit of the group and would be defended in battle until the last.

The Navy During the period of the empire the navy had four permanent fleets at its disposal, two in Italy (at Cumae near Naples, and at Ravenna), one on the North Sea, and one on the Black Sea.

Before the Year 1000

This chapter examines the long centuries during which a new social and political order developed in Europe after the fall of the Roman Empire. The fragmentation of the Germanic forces who invaded the empire made it very difficult to keep the vast new territories and disparate peoples under control. In fact, when the campaign for the conquest of Italy was launched from Byzantium (then capital of the Eastern Roman Empire), the initial successes were considerable. But Byzantium too had problems in the East and could not involve itself thoroughly in the defense of the West. Despite Rome's distraction, the Ostrogoths and later the Franks decided to seek a reconciliation with the Roman world, which they accomplished through mass conversion to Christianity and agreements with the pope, the only authority who could officially sanction a new central power. Thus the Holy Roman Empire was born. But the price of this political operation, for Rome, was her definitive detachment from the orthodox East.

The Fief The new territorial and political unit into which the German empire was subdivided was the fief, with which the emperor, and then the king in France and En-

gland, invested their faithful dignitaries. But when the fief became hereditary, a lawful aristocracy was formed which was often in conflict with the central power; these conflicts created serious dynastic problems, along with related political and military tensions.

Clearly distinguished from the feudal castle, the towns too demanded independence and claimed rights of their own. The sovereigns allied themselves alternately with the towns and with the feudal lords to suppress the excessive liberties of the former or the demands and plots of the latter. The political framework was thus very unstable, and armed clashes were frequent.

The Romanesque Style The new style in art that became widespread in buildings and in carved or painted decoration was called Romanesque: from Roman taste it retained a grandiosity (as in the basilicas) and a love of realistic representation, while from the Oriental tradition it took a feeling for color (as in the glowing mosaics) and minute detail, and a static quality in depiction. And the barbarian world added a more primitive and spontaneous feeling for creativity which, though unrelated to the golden proportions of the classical world, was richly imaginative and full of new images.

The Fair Fairs created centers of trade, which contributed to the development and wealth of medieval cities. The growth of these centers in turn stimulated trade. The most important fairs were the large-scale markets set up on special occasions. Usually they were linked to religious festivals with large gatherings of people, and on these occasions trade was tax free. The fairs regulated their own trade in accordance with negotiating laws set up on the basis of supply and demand.

Saddle and Stirrup Even in the ancient world people did not ride bareback; a covering was used, possibly of hide, although the Germanic tribes considered such a covering to be a sign of softness. But real saddles—that is, upholstered seats—made their appearance among the Romans as late as the fourth century A.D.

Before the development of the stirrup, horsemen used leather rings to support their feet, but these were clearly not very efficient and could also be quite dangerous. The rigid metal stirrup was seen for the first time in Europe among the Avars, horsemen who came from the steppes of Asia around A.D. 560. In northern Europe the stirrup first appeared in the eighth century.

The custom of shoeing draft animals dates back to the Romans. However, in the early Middle Ages many animals still went unshod.

The Free Communes

This chapter deals with the historical period around 1200, when medieval society reached its period of greatest splendor. One of the causes of the eventual decline was the Black Death, which raged throughout Europe for about twenty years in the first half of the fourteenth century.

Population A few statistics indicate an increase in population after the year 1000 until the Black Death exerted its influence. In 1086 there were 1,200,000 people living in the English shires, and in 1340 there were 2,355,000, practically double the number. In the German region between the Rhine and the Moselle, particularly rich and fertile, the population actually increased tenfold between the tenth and thirteenth centuries. In four centuries, in Germany, at least 2,500 towns came into existence, some of which were to become the great cities we know today. This is a spectacular example of the transformation of an agricultural society into an urban one.

The phenomenon of city growth was widespread. In 1200 Paris had about 100,000 inhabitants, which swelled to a good 240,000 by 1300. The small island on the Seine, called Lutetia Parisiorum by the Romans, thus became a great capital. Florence too doubled in size in the same period, as did the Flemish cities of Bruges and Ghent.

The rights that the developing communes demanded and obtained from the central authorities were the following: the right to hold a market regularly; the right to devise their own systems of weights and measures; the right to try their own citizens in local courts according to their own laws and ordinances; and the right to bear arms. This last was particularly significant, since it might also be used to rebel against authority. Legal appeals to the emperor or the king were always allowed. When the sovereign visited the towns he held court, settling controversies and delivering his own definitive sentences.

Civil Guard   Groups of armed men were needed to defend the cities and keep order within them. All male citizens, except for men in religious orders, had to serve at arms and take their turn in the civil guard. Many towns also had a night watch.

Cathedrals and Churches   More than any other monument, cathedrals expressed the degree of economic and technological development of medieval society, as well as the central position occupied by Christian ideals in medieval society, however poorly they might be lived up to in practice. Cathedrals were used only for the great festivals, while day-to-day religious activities took place in small neighborhood communities, all of which had their own churches. Even today old European towns and cities have dozens of small churches and oratories, sometimes just a few yards from one another.

Public Services   The Church was a many-sided organization, and its presence was felt in all town activities. In particular it concerned itself with all activities regarded as works of charity, such as lodging pilgrims (in hospices) or caring for the sick (in hospitals and sanatoria). Christian thought accepted and took notice of suffering, just as it valued the solidarity of those who alleviated it.

Guilds   The Middle Ages had a corporate economy, that is, one based on the association of people who practiced a single given activity. Rather than protect the various categories of workers, as modern trade unions do, each guild tended to favor the development of its own art, to the benefit of all ranks involved. But guilds were extremely class-bound, with sharp distinctions between apprentices, journeymen, and masters, who were also differentiated on the basis of their wealth. Guild headquarters and merchants' meeting places might have two separate rooms for the

weddings of their members, one first-class and another second-class. In a sense, the guilds also represent the beginnings of capitalism, in that they recognized the importance of wealth invested in labor. Furthermore, the bosses were masters in their own craft or trade and did not regard manual work as demeaning. Only the feudal aristocracy did not engage in any physical work, except for hunting and bearing arms.

Universities   One of the most important medieval institutions was the university, a permanent structure where an educated community had the space and means to engage in all branches of study. Law, based on Roman law, was considered a particularly important area of study, as was medicine, which reinstated the medical tradition of the Greeks and Arabs through the famous School of Salerno. Christian theology was another dominant field of study, particulary under the influence of St. Thomas Aquinas. The oldest universities were at Bologna, Paris, Cambridge, and Salamanca (founded in 1100, 1150, 1229, and 1243, respectively). Exchanges between universities were common and many scholars traveled from one to another to complete their studies: they were called *clerici vagantes*, or wandering scholars.

Water Power   The following description of the river running through the abbey at Clairvaux may give us an idea of the uses of this particular source of energy: "The river enters the abbey through the conduit along which it is channeled. It springs up first in the mill, where it is used to grind the grain under the weight of the wheels and to work the delicate sifter which separates the flour from the bran. Then it flows into the building nearby and fills the caldron where it is heated for the preparation of the monks' beer. . . . Then it passes to the fulling machines which are situated just beyond the mill. In the mill it prepares the food for the monks, and then its task is to contribute to the making of their habits. . . . Then it enters the tannery, where it devotes much effort and care to preparing the materials necessary for the monks' sandals. . . . Then it divides into so many small streams and, on its busy way, flows through the various sections, everywhere seeking out those who require its services for whatever purpose, cooking, turning, crushing, watering, washing. . . . Finally, to earn the fullest thanks and so that nothing shall be left undone, it carries away the refuse and leaves everything well and truly clean."

Monarchs Great and Small

This chapter deals with the centuries between the fifteenth and seventeenth, when the absolute power of the reigning dynasties was consolidated, and when the free cities developed into dukedoms and principalities.

The Republics   The Republic of Venice, hitherto devoted solely to maritime trade, but concerned now at having no secure territory beyond the coast, built itself a vast dominion on the mainland. As long as maritime interests remained concentrated in the Mediterranean, Venice continued to increase its power, carrying off triumphant victories against the Saracens and creating its own settlements in Crete, Cyprus, and other strategic islands. But with the opening up of the Atlantic routes, another republic, Holland, began its century-long sway over the seas. The seventeenth century was the golden age of Dutch economic and cultural development. After a long and arduous struggle to free itself from Spanish domination, the seven provinces of the Low Countries united, setting up their own republican institutions and statutes. Here the mercantile bourgeoisie became the ruling class. The city of Amsterdam grew from a small port on the Amstel River to a great capital, whose planned development was the finest example of town planning in history.

Renaissance The term *renaissance*, which means "rebirth," is used to describe the great period of cultural revival which affected all branches of study and the arts from 1400 onward. It is linked to Humanism, a rediscovery of the Greco-Roman world in philosophy and literature. In Florence, within only a few decades, three great artists, Brunelleschi, Donatello, and Masaccio gave new life to architecture, sculpture, and painting, respectively. Theirs was a reaction to medieval art, which was now contemptuously described as Gothic.

The Navigators The new burst of cultural life and man's newfound faith in himself contributed largely to the successes in the discovery of new continents. The spirit of adventure led brave men to cross the oceans, as it moved the explorer Ferdinand Magellan to attempt the circumnavigation of the globe.

The Galley, Sailing Ship, and Galleon The galley was the traditional warship of the Mediterranean. It had twenty-five to eighty benches on one side and each bench seated three oarsmen, each of whom used a separate oar. It had a single mast with a lateen sail, so that the rowers could rest when a favorable wind was blowing. When there were no volunteers for this work, the oarsmen were drawn from among criminals or prisoners of war. They were bound to their bench throughout the voyage and, if necessary, were encouraged with wine and the whip. There were also small galleys, called galliots, brigantines, and frigates.

The mercantile galley was larger and could carry up to 250 tons of merchandise. It had three masts and used oars only in cases of emergency. It had cannon in its bows, and was regarded as a very safe craft, so that the merchants could actually avoid insuring their goods.

The Mediterranean galley was not suited to sailing in the Atlantic, which required boats with round hulls; these could carry men and provisions for the longer voyage. The masts had several sails (at least three on three-masters), not to catch the wind better, but because a variety of smaller sails made the ship easier to control, as well as safer in the open sea. Surprisingly, the ships on which Columbus and Magellan embarked on their historic voyages were unsatisfactory. Of the five ships acquired in Spain for the circumnavigation of the globe, a chronicler wrote in 1518: "They are very old and patched-up, and I would not willingly travel on them even to the Canary Islands, because their sides are soft as butter."

The galleon was developed by the Portuguese as a large warship, and this model was used by Spaniards and En-glishmen to build the powerful military fleets that were to clash in the English Channel, with disastrous results for Spain. The galleon was armed with heavy cannon and was very swift, despite its considerable tonnage.

Sleeves In the sixteenth century Italian fashion began to use the double, interchangeable sleeve. Indeed, people sometimes had many pairs of sleeves, which could be put on several garments, providing a number of different combinations. This custom gave rise to the Italian expression "That's another pair of sleeves," meaning "That's quite a different matter."

Sleeves and stockings were sometimes slashed in strips to reveal brightly colored silk linings through the slits. This fashion for "slashing" seems to have been introduced by *Landsknechte*, German mercenary soldiers.

Gunpowder Gunpowder was introduced to Europe in the thirteenth century. A mixture of saltpeter, sulphur, and charcoal, it was invented in China and brought to Europe possibly by way of Byzantium. However, the application of gunpowder to firearms was a completely European invention. The mixture was made in the right proportions with mortar and pestle. The powder was kept damp to avoid explosions, although in fact these were frequent anyway, as they still are today when people experiment with fireworks.

Soldiers of Fortune In the sixteenth century bands of soldiers, led by bold captains, were organized. War became a profession. Needless to say, mercenaries chose the flag that paid the most money.

Fortifications The use of artillery brought about modifications in the concepts of military engineering, adapting them to the explosive power of new weapons. Cities were no longer defended by towers and walls, but by powerful ramparts.

Revolution!

The eighteenth century was the Age of Enlightenment, characterized by a rational and "modern" outlook that was in total contrast to that of the previous era, known for the wide support of absolute monarchy and resistance to the spread of knowledge.

England Throughout the eighteenth century England was the testing ground for modern developments in trade, agriculture, and industry. Many experiments were carried out there in a variety of areas of technology and production. Because of the widespread application of coal-powered steam engines, England became the leader in the Industrial Revolution, with half a century's advance over other northern European nations.

The Lunar Society Toward the end of the eighteenth century, a strange society was founded in Birmingham, England. Its members, principally doctors, philosophers, inventors, and scholars, were involved in science and industrial production and included such men as Matthew Boulton, James Watt, and Erasmus Darwin (grandfather of the naturalist who put forward the case for evolution). The name Lunar Society came from the fact that the group met every month on the Monday nearest the full moon. Meetings began at two in the afternoon and in the evening the members dined together. They chose the full moon so they could return home by moonlight. The date of the meeting was announced roughly as follows: "You are reminded that the next full moon will be Saturday, March 3." Without publicly advertising their activities, this group of industrialists, inventors, and philosophers transformed science and technology in Britain.

Architecture War damage involved architects and engineers in large-scale works of reconstruction. Massive movement into cities and towns created strong incentives for builders and community planners to seek alternative solutions to mere random expansion. Satellite towns were built to reduce concentration in the great cities, and there were plans to design linear cities along the great linking arteries of roads and railways.

The intellectual movement that dominated architectural planning and urban design in the twentieth century was known as rationalism, for the very reasons that it tended toward a rational and functional solution of serious housing and urban problems, and that it partially abandoned the demands of civic grandeur and symbolism. But in the new age of prosperity, such demands are once more making themselves felt.

Energy Initially, internal combustion engines powered by diesel fuel were used to produce electrical energy. These motors would drive turbines, which in turn drove the armature around magnets to produce alternating current.

Another way of fueling electric power stations was to use the mechanical energy produced by the flow of water in canals and waterfalls. This was a renewable and theoretically inexhaustible source, which was also free and nonpolluting. The disadvantage was that power stations had to be built where geographical conditions allowed, while lines had to be laid to transport the current, and this at great expense. There was therefore a shift to thermoelectric stations fueled by oil. These are still in use; they can be built anywhere and the fuel can be stored.

Apart from the fact that oil is a resource that may be exhausted, not centuries from now but in mere decades, the dependence of many European countries on other countries that produce oil has recently persuaded people to build nuclear power stations, which make use of atomic energy.

The real challenge is to produce electrical energy at a cost low enough to keep down the cost of manufacturing other products. But it is clearly shortsighted to allow a purely economic viewpoint to dictate in these matters, if cheaper energy means atmospheric pollution and the danger of radioactive contamination of vast areas. It of course makes better sense to discover and employ clean forms of alternative energy.

Off-the-Peg Clothes It was in Paris, center of fashion and elegance, after the French Revolution, that the first shops selling cheap ready-made clothes opened. Fear of this trend resulted in the development of *haute couture*, or high fashion, during the time of Napoleon; this was inspired in part by paintings by Jacques-Louis David, depicting scenes from the Roman world.

The Age of Progress

This was the age of coal and steel, of industrial production, of railways—the nineteenth century, a time when faith in the use of machines created enormous expectations.

The Risorgimento One of the most important movements for national unity and liberation from foreign powers was the Italian Risorgimento, which gave Italy the ideal impetus to regain her identity as a nation after so many centuries. This period saw the wars of independence against the Austro-Hungarian Empire, which was occupying Lombardy and the Veneto, and also the famous "Expedition of the Thousand," led by Giuseppe Garibaldi to unite northern and southern Italy, a union sealed by the occupation of Rome in 1870.

Slum Clearance The type of operation carried out in the nineteenth century on crumbling, dirty town centers was known as "slum clearance." Though the avowed aim was to do away with unhealthy districts, these operations were often carried out very clumsily, destroying whole neighborhoods without solving the housing problem. One spectacular undertaking of this kind, carried out by the state with the introduction of expropriation laws, was performed in Naples.

Impressionism There was a turning point in the field of art, too, in the second half of the nineteenth century. A completely new movement, at first contemptuously called impressionism, emerged. The first exhibitions of painters whom we regard today as geniuses, such as Renoir and Manet, were attended by people who went there to mock or express their outrage. With impressionism, modern art was born.

Feminism In all fields, nineteenth-century ideas expressed a tendency toward renewal and a demand for freedom and justice. Women began to speak out against their state of subjection and above all their exclusion from places of learning and public life. These were the forerunners of the suffragettes, who fought for women's right to vote. Universal suffrage, the right of all citizens, male and female alike, to vote, is still not a reality in all countries.

The Turn of the Twentieth Century

Futurism The first decade of the twentieth century was infused with a desire for change, which seems to be the fruit of expectations and faith in the future that were typical of the nineteenth century. The cultural movement that most notably shows this spirit is futurism, with its exaltation of speed, the machine, and great human undertaking. But the stirrings of doubt and unease expressed by other philosophical and artistic movements, such as French and German expressionism, imply the birth of a more critical awareness in Europe and a widespread fear that progress also carried within it the seeds of destruction and death. The great European tragedy of the two world wars forced people to reconsider the limits of development, to think about possible negative effects, and plan the future in more rational terms.

Guide to Periods and Subjects

	The Ancient World — from the dawn of history to the Hellenistic period	One Great Empire Alone — the Roman Empire around A.D. 100	Before the Year 1000 — from the fall of the Roman Empire to feudalism	The Free Communes — around 1200	Monarchs Great and Small — from 1400 to 1600	Revolution! — around 1700	The Age of Progress — around 1800	The Turn of the Twentieth Century — around 1900
page	8	26	44	62	80	98	116	134
page	10	28	46	64	82	100	118	136
page	12	30	48	66	84	102	120	138
page	14	32	50	68	86	104	122	140
page	16	34	52	70	88	106	124	142
page	18	36	54	72	90	108	126	144
page	20	38	56	74	92	110	128	146
page	22	40	58	76	94	112	130	148
page	24	42	60	78	96	114	132	150